About This Book

Why is this topic important?

As the environment in which organizations operate has grown more competitive and demanding, the need for a structured approach to developing leaders has increased markedly. Many different organizations and the development professionals who work in and with them are looking for ideas about how to develop talent throughout their organizations. They want a development approach that closely connects to their particular organization's business needs so that they can create value and sustainability.

What can you achieve with this book?

The purpose of this book is to help you organize your thinking and planning for maintaining a leadership pipeline in your organization. CCL's Developing Leadership Talent (DLT) approach is intended to prompt a professional examination of those needs and ensure that you address the issues most relevant to success. This book will be most useful to human resource or organization development professionals responsible for designing leadership development and talent management strategies in their organizations. Consultants who help organizations design such strategies will also find useful information in these pages.

In contemporary organizations, many executives and managers at different levels of leadership are responsible for implementing development strategies. Although we do not intend this book to serve that audience directly, it does provide an overview of expectations and procedures that can aid their understanding and so help them implement and support those strategies.

How is the book organized?

The components of our DLT approach can help you build an effective leadership development process for your organization. Each chapter goes into detail about the dimensions and uses of each element, with concrete suggestions for using these principles, stories of other organizations and how they have used these principles, and worksheets and other exercises to involve you in your own program design.

We considered several points in constructing CCL's DLT program. One, we placed a strong emphasis on the link between business need and development. Also, we took into account that readers may use our approach to customize the programs they had already designed; so it's not necessary to use the components of the DLT approach sequentially (even though you could start at the beginning and work through if you were building from scratch and wanted to integrate your program activities). We also applied and emphasized CCL's development framework (assessment, challenge, and support), as we have found it to be a flexible, powerful means of addressing the question of how you help others develop leadership capacity.

The ideas, strategies, and tools that we suggest in this book are broad enough to apply to a variety of situations. And we emphasize that DLT is an approach—it is not a complex, overarching system for talent management. Our experience is that the people who attend the DLT program, like our intended readers, are looking for a simple organizing framework around which they can design their development initiatives.

This book is based on what we have learned from constructing and teaching the DLT program. We think it captures our thinking about ways to develop a process to implement development initiatives that respond to the strategic imperatives of your organization.

About Pfeiffer

Pfeiffer serves the professional development and hands-on resource needs of training and human resource practitioners and gives them products to do their jobs better. We deliver proven ideas and solutions from experts in HR development and HR management, and we offer effective and customizable tools to improve workplace performance. From novice to seasoned professional, Pfeiffer is the source you can trust to make yourself and your organization more successful.

Essential Knowledge Pfeiffer produces insightful, practical, and comprehensive materials on topics that matter the most to training and HR professionals. Our Essential Knowledge resources translate the expertise of seasoned professionals into practical, how-to guidance on critical workplace issues and problems. These resources are supported by case studies, worksheets, and job aids and are frequently supplemented with CD-ROMs, websites, and other means of making the content easier to read, understand, and use.

Essential Tools Pfeiffer's Essential Tools resources save time and expense by offering proven, ready-to-use materials—including exercises, activities, games, instruments, and assessments—for use during a training or team-learning event. These resources are frequently offered in looseleaf or CD-ROM format to facilitate copying and customization of the material.

Pfeiffer also recognizes the remarkable power of new technologies in expanding the reach and effectiveness of training. While e-hype has often created whizbang solutions in search of a problem, we are dedicated to bringing convenience and enhancements to proven training solutions. All our e-tools comply with rigorous functionality standards. The most appropriate technology wrapped around essential content yields the perfect solution for today's on-the-go trainers and human resource professionals.

Essential resources for training and HR professionals

ABOUT THE CENTER FOR CREATIVE LEADERSHIP

The Center for Creative Leadership (CCL) is a top-ranked, global provider of executive education that develops better leaders through its exclusive focus on leadership education and research. Founded in 1970 as a nonprofit, educational institution, CCL helps clients worldwide cultivate creative leadership—the capacity to achieve more than imagined by thinking and acting beyond boundaries— through an array of programs, products, and other services.

Ranked in the top ten in the *Financial Times* annual executive education survey, CCL is headquartered in Greensboro, North Carolina, with campuses in Colorado Springs, Colorado; San Diego, California; Brussels, Belgium; and Singapore. Supported by more than five hundred faculty members and staff, it works annually with more than twenty thousand leaders and three thousand organizations. In addition, sixteen Network Associates around the world offer selected CCL programs and assessments.

CCL draws strength from its nonprofit status and educational mission, which provide unusual flexibility in a world where quarterly profits often drive thinking and direction. It has the freedom to be objective, wary of short-term trends, and motivated foremost by its mission—hence its substantial and sustained investment in leadership research. Although CCL's work is always grounded in a strong foundation of research, it focuses on achieving a beneficial impact in the real world. Its efforts are geared to be practical and action oriented, helping leaders and their organizations more effectively achieve their goals and vision. The desire to transform learning and ideas into action provides the impetus for CCL's programs, assessments, publications, and services.

CAPABILITIES

CCL's activities encompass leadership education, knowledge generation and dissemination, and building a community centered on leadership. CCL is broadly recognized for excellence in executive education, leadership development, and innovation by sources such as *BusinessWeek, Financial Times, The New York Times,* and *The Wall Street Journal.*

OPEN-ENROLLMENT PROGRAMS

Fourteen open-enrollment courses are designed for leaders at all levels, as well as people responsible for leadership development and training at their organizations. This portfolio offers distinct choices for participants seeking a particular learning environment or type of experience. Some programs are structured specifically around small group activities, discussion, and personal reflection, while others offer hands-on opportunities through business simulations, artistic exploration, team-building exercises, and new-skills practice. Many of these programs offer private one-on-one sessions with a feedback coach.

For a complete listing of programs, visit http://www.ccl.org/programs.

CUSTOMIZED PROGRAMS

CCL develops tailored educational solutions for more than one hundred client organizations around the world each year. Through this applied practice, CCL structures and delivers programs focused on specific leadership development needs within the context of defined organizational challenges, including innovation, the merging of cultures, and the development of a broader pool of leaders. The objective is to help organizations develop, within their own cultures, the leadership capacity they need to address challenges as they emerge.

Program details are available online at http://www.ccl.org/custom.

COACHING

CCL's suite of coaching services is designed to help leaders maintain a sustained focus and generate increased momentum toward achieving their goals. These coaching alternatives vary in depth and duration and serve a variety of needs, from helping an executive sort through career and life issues to working with an organization to integrate coaching into its internal development process. Our coaching offerings, which can supplement program attendance or be customized for specific individual or team needs, are based on our ACS model of assessment, challenge, and support.

Learn more about CCL's coaching services at http://www.ccl.org/coaching.

ASSESSMENT AND DEVELOPMENT RESOURCES

CCL pioneered 360-degree feedback and believes that assessment provides a solid foundation for learning, growth, and transformation and that development truly happens when an individual recognizes the need to change. CCL offers a broad selection of assessment tools, online resources, and simulations that can help individuals, teams, and organizations increase their self-awareness, facilitate their own learning, enable their development, and enhance their effectiveness.

CCL's assessments are profiled at http://www.ccl.org/assessments.

PUBLICATIONS

The theoretical foundation for many of our programs, as well as the results of CCL's extensive and often groundbreaking research, can be found in the scores of publications issued by CCL Press and through the Center's alliance with Jossey-Bass, a Wiley imprint. Among these are landmark works, such as *Breaking the Glass Ceiling* and *The Lessons of Experience,* as well as quick-read guidebooks focused on core aspects of leadership. CCL publications provide insights and practical advice to help individuals become more effective leaders, develop leadership training within organizations, address issues of change and diversity, and build the systems and strategies that advance leadership collectively at the institutional level.

A complete listing of CCL publications is available at http://www.ccl.org/publications.

LEADERSHIP COMMUNITY

To ensure that the Center's work remains focused, relevant, and important to the individuals and organizations it serves, CCL maintains a host of networks, councils, and learning and virtual communities that bring together alumni, donors, faculty, practicing leaders, and thought leaders from around the globe. CCL also forges relationships and alliances with individuals, organizations, and associations that share its values and mission. The energy, insights, and support from these relationships help shape and sustain CCL's educational and research practices and provide its clients with an added measure of motivation and inspiration as they continue their lifelong commitment to leadership and learning.

To learn more, visit http://www.ccl.org/community.

RESEARCH

CCL's portfolio of programs, products, and services is built on a solid foundation of behavioral science research. The role of research at CCL is to advance the understanding of leadership and to transform learning into practical tools for participants and clients. CCL's research is the hub of a cycle that transforms knowledge into applications and applications into knowledge, thereby illuminating the way organizations think about and enact leadership and leader development.

Find out more about current research initiatives at http://www.ccl.org/research.

For additional information about CCL, please visit http://www.ccl.org or call Client Services at (336) 545-2810.

Developing Leadership Talent

David Berke
Michael E. Kossler
Michael Wakefield

Pfeiffer
A Wiley Imprint
www.pfeiffer.com

Published by Pfeiffer
A Wiley Imprint
989 Market Street, San Francisco, CA 94103-1741 www.pfeiffer.com

Library of Congress Cataloging-in-Publication Data

Berke, David.
    Developing leadership talent / David Berke, Michael E. Kossler, Michael Wakefield.
       p. cm.
    Includes bibliographical references and index.
    ISBN 978-0-470-17702-0 (pbk.)
    1. Executives—Training of. 2. Executive ability. 3. Leadership. I. Kossler, Michael E.
II. Wakefield, Michael. III. Title.
    HD30.4.B482 2008
    658.4'092—dc22
                                                  2008003846

Acquiring Editor: Lisa Shannon
Director of Development: Kathleen Dolan Davies
Marketing Manager: Brian Grimm
Production Editor: Michael Kay

Editor: Rebecca Taff
Assistant Editor: Marisa Kelley
Manufacturing Supervisor: Becky Morgan

Printed in the United States of America
Printing   10 9 8 7 6 5 4 3 2 1

CONTENTS

PREFACE

CCL's interest in developing leadership talent in organizations dates at least to 1989, when it offered two programs: Designing Systems for Executive Development and Tools for Developing Successful Executives. Since then, CCL has published several books on the topic, the most relevant being *How to Design an Effective System for Developing Managers and Executives* in 1996.

Although not a direct line, those experiences and the knowledge gained are context within which CCL has created its current public program: Developing Leadership Talent: Strategies and Tools (DLT). We designed the approach at the heart of DLT to enable development professionals to fashion a sensible, coherent process for building leadership strength in their organizations. That approach is the basis for this book.

The authors want to acknowledge the groundbreaking work of Maxine Dalton and Cindy McCauley and the positive influence it had on our thinking and the evolution of the DLT framework. They also express their thanks to clients and classroom participants for keeping the material grounded in reality, to the CCL library and librarians for their assistance and resourcefulness, and to their editors Pete Scisco and Leslie Stephen for their patience, organization, and for asking good questions and making this book better.

In particular, David thanks his co-authors for the stimulating conversations that have resulted from this endeavor, and he thanks Nancy—just because.

Michael Kossler thanks Sharon, Rachel, and Sarah. Without their patience and understanding he would never have had time to complete this project.

Michael Wakefield also thanks his co-authors for their teaching and learning together, and acknowledges Joyce, Niki, and Dylan, the most important teachers in his life.

The Talent Imperative

Recently, a representative of a major automobile manufacturer told us that he wanted to know what the best practices were for developing the leadership talent in his organization. The squeeze is on for the auto companies, he said. What kinds of approaches and practices, he asked, had the best chance for success?

A home-improvement company representative came to us with a similar request. What advice could we give her about programs and development approaches that would provide sustainability and continuous improvement for her company?

These are just two examples of the comments we often receive from professionals who are responsible for developing executives and managers in organizations. The importance of developing leadership talent is not new, but it rarely has been more important than now. The impact of demographic shifts described in *The War for Talent* (Michaels, Handfield-Jones, & Axelrod, 2001) are emerging—not just in North America but globally. When the older workers leave, there simply will not be enough trained managers and executives for some time (Coy & Ewing, 2007).

Not only is the business environment increasingly competitive, but there are also other challenges. These include mergers, acquisitions, and regular restructuring that, at a minimum, create disarray in the corporate cultures that might otherwise groom managers for leadership positions.

One critical way for organizations to achieve competitive advantage is for them to create an approach to recruiting and retaining high-quality managerial talent that includes a focus on developing the kinds of skills and behavior that tie directly to the needs of the business (Dalton & Hollenbeck, 1996). In fact, a CEO survey in *Chief Executive* magazine (Haapaniemi, 2002) reported that most

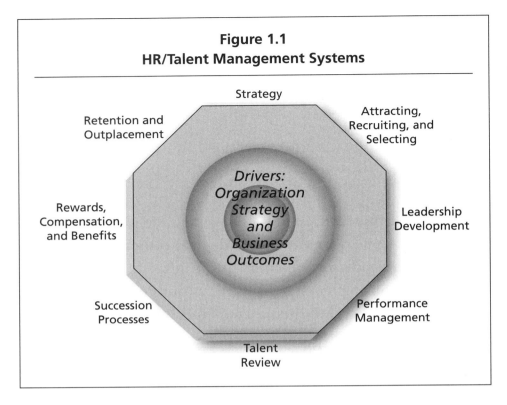

Figure 1.1
HR/Talent Management Systems

Strategy

Retention and
Outplacement

Attracting,
Recruiting, and
Selecting

Rewards,
Compensation,
and Benefits

*Drivers:
Organization
Strategy
and
Business
Outcomes*

Leadership
Development

Succession
Processes

Performance
Management

Talent
Review

of its respondents (78.6 percent) see the ability to develop leaders as crucial to achieving competitive advantage.

As the focus on people (or the lack of people) has increased, talent management has emerged as a particular way of managing an organization's human resources. It shifts the emphasis toward proactive management of the "talent pipeline."

Developing leadership talent falls within the context of talent management. We define talent management as an integrated approach to recruiting, developing, and retaining talent. Within these three categories, talent management systems often include some or all of the following: recruiting and selecting; performance management; leadership development; talent review; succession processes; rewards, compensation, and benefits; retention and outplacement (see Figure 1.1).

TALENT MANAGEMENT

Our work overlaps with and reflects talent management best practices. According to a 2004 report published by the American Productivity and Quality Center

(APQC), the most successful organizations in terms of managing talent link their senior leadership, human resources, and line management in a development process that drives improved performance. The report cites Capital One Finance, Celanese AG, Coca-Cola HBC, the Internal Revenue Service, and other organizations as examples.

APQC identified eight themes among the best practices implemented by successful organizations to attract, develop, and retain critical organizational talent.

1. They define *talent management* broadly.

2. They integrate the elements of talent management into a comprehensive system.

3. They focus talent management on the most highly valued talent.

4. Their CEOs and senior executives are committed to and invest their time in talent-management activities.

5. They build competency models to create a shared understanding of the skills and behaviors that the organization needs and values in employees.

6. They monitor talent to identify current or potential future talent gaps (see Figure 1.2 for an example).

7. They excel at recruiting, identifying, developing, and retaining talent, as well as managing performance.

8. They regularly evaluate the results of their talent management efforts (see Figure 1.3 for an example).

MISCUES IN DEVELOPING LEADERSHIP TALENT

The 2002 *Chief Executive* study mentioned earlier shows that many of the organizations surveyed lack a formal process for leadership development. By not having a formal or systematic approach, organizations make it difficult if not impossible to leverage their investment in development.

The authors of *The War for Talent* report a number of problems in organizations that do not do a good job of developing talent. For example, a majority of corporate officers said their inability to develop their people into great executives was a major obstacle to strengthening the talent pool and that their organizations did not develop people quickly and effectively.

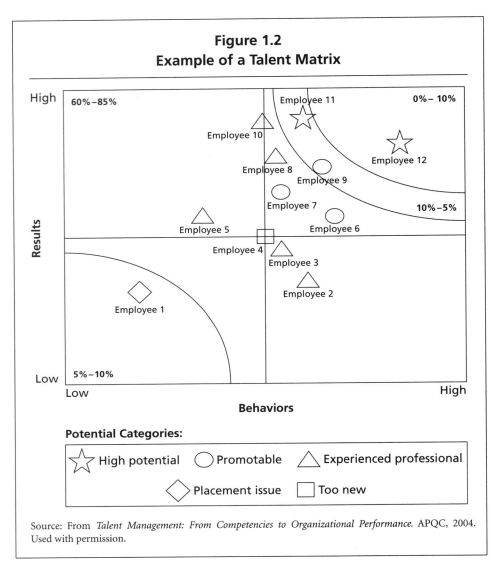

Figure 1.2
Example of a Talent Matrix

Source: From *Talent Management: From Competencies to Organizational Performance*. APQC, 2004. Used with permission.

The authors also report that managers who feel their companies develop them poorly are five times more likely to leave than people who feel their companies develop them well, and that a majority of managers who intend to leave their current employers in the next two years cite insufficient development and learning opportunities as critical or very important reasons for leaving.

Recent CCL research (see Table 1.1) reveals some of the difference between the skills that leaders have developed and the skills that support their organizations'

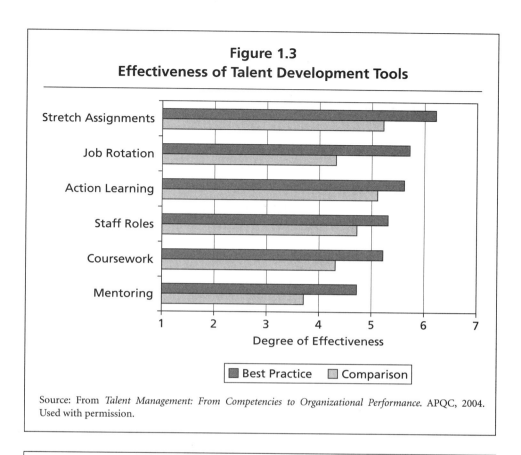

Figure 1.3
Effectiveness of Talent Development Tools

Degree of Effectiveness

■ Best Practice   □ Comparison

Source: From *Talent Management: From Competencies to Organizational Performance.* APQC, 2004. Used with permission.

Table 1.1
Six Most Important Leadership Attributes and Strengths

Attributes Critical to Strategic Success	Strengths Developed Among Leaders
1 Leading People	Respecting Individuals
2 Strategic Planning	Doing Whatever It Takes
3 Resourceful	Culturally Adaptable
4 Being a Quick Learner	Being a Quick Learner
5 Inspiring Commitment	Composed
6 Participative Management	Compassion and Sensitivity

Adapted from the Center for Creative Leadership's "Understanding the Leadership Gap" research project, as reported in *LEADAsia*, 2007.

strategy. Important leadership dimensions are not being developed, which can affect an organization's ability to create leadership capacity.

THE DLT APPROACH

In this book we focus on the intersection of talent management and leadership development. We want to help you think through how you can build and maintain a leadership pipeline in your organization and link that to your organization's business needs.

CCL's Developing Leadership Talent (DLT) approach is intended to ensure that you address the relevant issues at both an individual and organizational level (see Figure 1.4).

Notice the two-level ACS model in the middle of Figure 1.4. ACS represents CCL's fundamental development framework. "A" stands for *assessment*. Effective development requires a baseline measure of the current state. This sometimes

---

Figure 1.4
Developing Leadership Talent: An Approach to the Process

Ongoing Evaluation
- Determine effectiveness of development system on individuals and organization
- Guide adjustment to maintain effective development system

Business Strategy/Organizational Needs
- Core for organization's Vision/Mission
- Specific to current and future business challenges

Implementation
The processes used in a systematic way that lead to ongoing development of specific levels of mastery for targeted competencies

Implications for Leadership
- Based on strategy: What will be different?
- Non-leadership issues

Organization

Individual

Development Strategies
Development methodologies used to attain desired level of mastery for identified competencies for identified target populations

Gap Analysis
Assessing difference between desired state and current state and determining resource investment to close gap

Leadership Competencies
Leadership skills and perspectives that drive desired culture, performance, and goal attainment

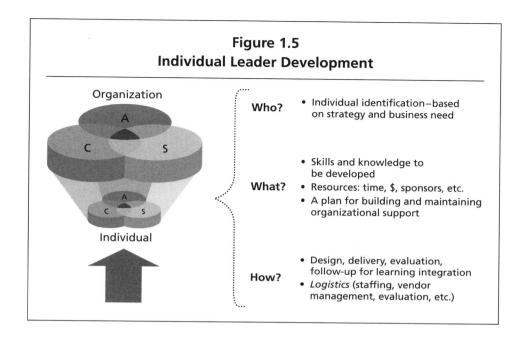

Figure 1.5
Individual Leader Development

Organization

Individual

Who?
- Individual identification–based on strategy and business need

What?
- Skills and knowledge to be developed
- Resources: time, $, sponsors, etc.
- A plan for building and maintaining organizational support

How?
- Design, delivery, evaluation, follow-up for learning integration
- *Logistics* (staffing, vendor management, evaluation, etc.)

can help reinforce a need for development. The "C" stands for *challenge*: Development requires moving beyond the comfort zone; it requires a stretch. Finally, the "S" stands for *support*: Development is much more likely to succeed if support is provided.

Figure 1.5 illustrates how ACS plays out at the individual level. Figure 1.6 illustrates ACS operating at the organizational level.

Returning to Figure 1.4, the DLT approach asks:

- What are the key challenges facing your organization over its next planning period—generally from two to five years?

- What must your leaders be able to do differently in order to implement your organization's business strategy? What capabilities do functions/departments in which these people work need to do more or less of, or do differently?

- What individual leader competencies and organization capabilities must be developed?

- Who will be developed: individuals, employee groups, functional units, or some other kind of organizational mix?

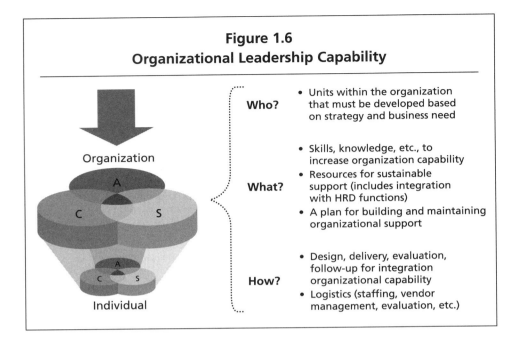

Figure 1.6
Organizational Leadership Capability

Organization

A

C S

A

C S

Individual

Who?
- Units within the organization that must be developed based on strategy and business need

What?
- Skills, knowledge, etc., to increase organization capability
- Resources for sustainable support (includes integration with HRD functions)
- A plan for building and maintaining organizational support

How?
- Design, delivery, evaluation, follow-up for integration organizational capability
- Logistics (staffing, vendor management, evaluation, etc.)

- What is the current skill level compared to the needed level?
- What development methodologies will you use and why? Will they build organizational capability?
- How will you implement your development initiative?
- How will you evaluate the impact of your leadership development initiative?

Each of these questions opens up its own line of investigation, its own rationale, and its own set of decisions. The DLT approach avoids setting out a complex, one-size-fits-all system. It is above all an organizing approach that gives professional developers parameters but maintains a great degree of flexibility.

Without a doubt, developing leadership capability and capacity requires time and effort to customize the appropriate developmental tools for your organization and to bring about necessary shifts in how individuals and groups do their work.

In *The Towers Perrin Talent Report: How Leading Organizations Manage Talent* (Towers Perrin, 2002), this business consulting firm examined twenty-two organizations, all of which confirmed that a long-term view of investing in people (development, training, coaching) was tied to sustaining profitability and growth.

Many of the executives CCL works with express the same view: when development is linked to real-world organizational challenges, success is long-lasting and well worth the time and effort. Those results have a cascading effect that benefits the current generation of managers and creates the opportunity for systemic development that benefits succeeding generations of managers.

IS YOUR ORGANIZATION READY TO DEVELOP LEADERSHIP TALENT?

You cannot build and implement an approach to developing leadership talent without ongoing support from your organization. Even organizations with a pro-development orientation can be unprepared to apply a fully systemic approach. Before you begin your own design, assess how ready your organization is to accept and support a systematic approach. You can measure readiness by considering your organization's most pressing strategic and organizational challenges, and using your analysis to narrow the areas of development in your plan. You can assess the organization through interviews, surveys, instruments, and your own observations. Use the Organizational Readiness Checklist (Exhibit 1.1) to record your findings.

As you assess your organization's readiness to accommodate and support the development of leadership talent, consider these questions.

- To what degree do I have full management support for sustainable leadership development?

- What are the challenges of getting senior management to actively participate and support leadership development?

- What development areas exist now and what areas are likely to reveal themselves later?

The answers to these questions will help guide you to a development approach that is aligned with your organization's view of developing leadership talent. By aligning yourself with its views, you are more likely to gain support for your approach.

Exhibit 1.1
Organizational Readiness Checklist

What is your organization's readiness to accommodate and support the development of leadership talent? The probes in this worksheet can help you gain a sense of the climate for introducing the DLT approach. This worksheet is not all-inclusive; if you have additional questions, add them to the worksheet to complete the picture.

Regarding the format:

- Column 1 (farthest to the left) lists the questions or probes for you to consider.

- Column 2 provides a rating on a scale of 1 to 10 (1 = does not address and 10 = completely satisfied) of the degree to which your organization already does this.

- Column 3 documents the reason for your rating by providing behavioral indicators.

- Column 4 rates how important this item is on a scale of 1 to 10 (1 = not important and 10 = high importance).

- Column 5 documents your reasons for giving the importance rating you gave the probe.

- Column 6 (farthest to the right) identifies who should be involved to increase the rating on this item.

1	2	3	4	5	6
Probe or Question	**Degree Already Satisfied (1–10)**	**Evidence (Observed/ Assessed)**	**Degree of Im- portance (1–10)**	**Evidence (Observed/ Assessed)**	**Stake-holders**
My organi- zation's phi- losophy and beliefs guide its decisions about leader development.					
My orga- nization's philosophy and beliefs are effective in guiding its decisions about leader development.					
My organi- zation's phi- losophy and beliefs will be effective in guiding future decisions about leader development.					
My orga- nization's development philosophy is integrated into its over- all strategy for talent management.					
Other:					

GETTING STARTED WITH DLT

When you finish the Organizational Readiness Checklist, you will have a general idea of whether you are ready to start or whether you first must build support.

In the following chapters, we discuss each part of the DLT approach. For some of the areas we address (business strategy/organizational needs, implications, leadership competency, target population and gap analysis, development methodologies, implementation, and evaluation), you may already have a solution in place. In that case, you may want to review our approach, compare it with your own work, and decide whether or not you want to alter what you currently are doing.

If your program for developing leadership talent has gaps or is in the early stages of design, you may want to use the DLT approach as a starting point for customizing a design that gains support in your organization and that aligns with its strategy. Our goal is to guide, but not create, your approach for addressing each of these critical areas.

One final note: The DLT approach is displayed in a linear form. That is because it mirrors the overall implementation sequence. However, while you might follow this overall sequence in implementation, it is useful to remember, for example, that:

- You must build support for the initiative and maintain support throughout the entire process and after, and

- Evaluation might be implemented at the conclusion of some work, but preparation for evaluation begins with clear desired goals and outcomes that are established at the beginning of any successful development initiative.

Business Strategy/ Organizational Needs

The primary purpose of developing leadership talent is to help an organization meet its strategic goals. Starting with a review of an organization's strategy documents often will provide a lens for identifying development needs at both the organizational and individual levels. Additionally, at the individual level, a direct link can be made to the leadership competencies your organization requires (more about that in Chapter 4).

Let's consider an example. A global electronics manufacturer grows quickly through acquisition. Until recently, the plants it had acquired operated autonomously. Due to competition, a new CEO decides to change the strategy and to reorganize the company. Now, the plants are organized globally by market segment. In such a scenario, just some of the challenges this strategic shift creates include:

- Clarity of vision and mission and effective communication of them
- Establishing a workable global structure for the different market segments
- Coordinating across once-autonomous plants and the functions within those plants
- Realigning relations with internal and external customers
- Dealing with multiple country cultures

Each of these challenges has leadership implications at both the organizational and individual levels. At the organizational level, there may be a need to create a sense of urgency to implement coordination mechanisms and processes across functions. Those mechanisms and processes may require individual leaders to perform differently. For example, within the various functions individuals will have to develop or refine skills in various competencies (say, negotiation and conflict management).

This is but one case showing how important it is for the organization's needs and challenges to factor into the development of leadership capacity.

The first step in linking leadership development with the organization's strategy is a process we call "assessing business and organizational needs." Here's how it works.

ASSESSING BUSINESS AND ORGANIZATIONAL NEEDS

Business issues drive the need for development. It is essential that you identify your organization's challenges in order to determine the leadership actions needed to address those challenges and the kind of development leaders will need so that they are capable of taking those actions. Knowing what your organization requires will help you refine your thoughts about what is necessary and what is not so important to address in terms of developing leadership talent. By carrying out a business and organizational needs assessment first, you will be able to directly link leader competencies with your organization's strategic direction.

WHAT TO LOOK FOR

There are some major considerations when approaching the assessment of business needs in the context of developing leadership talent. One, leadership development must be linked to and support the strategic direction of your organization. Two, development should address your organization's current and future external challenges. Third, it must take internal pressures into account. Any of those challenges can lead to strategic decisions that may require development or enhancement of leadership skills or knowledge. The following listing summarizes some of the challenges that organizations often face.

Common Organizational Challenges and Their Sources
Strategic Challenges
- Clarity of vision
- Support from board, shareholders, and employees

- Implementation issues
- Resistance to change

External Challenges
- The economy
- Competitive threats
- Client or consumer expectations
- Shareholder expectations
- Supplier issues
- Advances in technology
- Regulatory issues (employment, environment, privacy, for example)

Internal Challenges
- Merger or acquisition
- Reorganization
- Employee recruitment and retention
- Structure
- Information technology
- Globalization

WHERE TO LOOK

There are many ways to assess your company's business and organizational needs. These can include interviews with key executives, focus-group sessions, or organizational surveys. Exhibit 2.1 contains a series of questions that you could adapt for your own survey instrument or interview guide; questions 6 and 7 specifically address organizational challenges, but all are prompts for information useful throughout the DLT process.

We recommend that you interview a minimum of five senior-level leaders in your organization, ideally from different functions. Functions could include Sales, Manufacturing, Customer Service, Finance, Human Resources, etc. The data from these interviews can be used at various times throughout the DLT process to help shape your leadership development initiative for your organization.

Exhibit 2.1
Sample Business/Organizational Assessment Survey or Interview Guide

1. How would you describe our company's attitude toward leadership development?

2. Briefly explain how you think leadership development actually works in our company.

3. Name three to five leadership competencies you think are currently valued most in our company.

4. What makes you select these competencies?

5. How are these competencies emphasized in our company (encouraged, rewarded, etc.)?

6. What are the top business drivers, organizational issues, and marketplace challenges currently facing our company?

7. Given the drivers, issues, and challenges facing our company, what are the implications for leaders within our organization (at all levels, not just the executive level)?

8. In order to take action in response to these drivers, issues, and challenges, what skills (or competencies) will our leaders need to either possess or develop?

9. What do you think will happen if we don't have or develop these competencies in our current or future leaders?

10. Where and how did you acquire the necessary competencies for leadership in this company (prior to joining the company or since joining)? What were two or three events that made a lasting difference in the way you lead today?

11. If we were to prioritize our leadership development efforts, should we focus on a set of specific competencies for everyone or on a particular level or group within our company? What do you consider to be of critical importance?

12. Given our current business drivers, what development activity would have the greatest impact on enhancing our leadership capabilities as a competitive advantage?

One tactic we highly recommend for identifying organizational and business needs is to assemble a group of key leaders for a focus-group session. Typically, the focus group consists of eight to twelve individuals with different organizational responsibilities. In a session lasting from one and a half to two hours, you can gather key information using the steps outlined in Exhibit 2.2.

If your organization's CEO and direct reports participate in this focus group, you may need only one session to assess the organization's strategy implementation needs. If the top leaders do not participate, you may want to conduct two or three sessions with various groups of leaders to make sure you have gathered a wide range of data.

The support of the CEO is critical to creating a viable process for developing leadership talent. When the CEO has not participated in a focus-group discussion, it is critical that you review with him or her the challenges identified by the focus group(s) in order to ensure acceptance and agreement with the focus-group outcomes.

HOW TO ASSESS

There are many ways to organize and interpret the information you collect on your company's business and organizational needs. The Sample Business Strategy/Need Assessment Matrix (Exhibit 2.3) shows the way one company sized up the links between the organization's strategy and its leadership development processes.

We have included a blank Business Strategy/Need Assessment Worksheet (Exhibit 2.4) to help you organize the information you collect in your key executive interviews, focus-group sessions, organizational surveys, and other data gathering.

A final word: With the tactics, processes, and tools described in this chapter, you can gain some insight into your organization's strategy and the challenges it faces trying to implement it. From a leadership development perspective, your aim is to identify what leaders should do—what their actions should be—to help the organization achieve its strategic goals and address its critical business issues. You can use the checklist at the end of the chapter to ensure you have considered the key questions for this step in the DLT approach.

Whatever methods you use to assess your organization's challenges and its business needs, be sure to obtain the input of key leaders within your organization.

Exhibit 2.2
Key Leader Focus-Group Session

Step 1. Divide the large group into three small groups, and then assign each group one of three assessment focus points:

1. Challenges associated with implementing the organizational strategy

2. External business environment currently impacting the organizational strategy

3. Internal organizational challenges impacting the strategy

Each group brainstorms a list of challenges and then, through discussion, prioritizes and agrees on the top two to four. This part of the session can last about 20 minutes.

Step 2. Each small group makes a brief presentation of its list and the priorities it sets. These presentations frequently surface other challenges that were not identified by the group. This part of the session can last from 5 to 10 minutes.

Step 3. After each group has made its presentation, facilitate a discussion about the challenges facing implementation of the organization's strategy. Devote about 30 minutes to this part of the session.

Step 4. At the end of the discussion facilitated in Step 3, the entire group should agree on the top two to six challenges to implementing the organization's strategy. When the focus-group participants generally agree on the challenges facing their organization, this step is completed fairly quickly. Groups who lack this general agreement may require other techniques to reach agreement. Tools that you might use in this situation include triple ranking (each participant votes for three top choices) or technologies such as decision-making software.

Exhibit 2.3
Sample Business Strategy/Need Assessment Matrix

Probe/ Question	Degree Already Satis- fied (1–10)	Behavioral Indicators	Degree of Impor- tance (1–10)	Behavioral Indicators	Stake- holders
Our leadership development processes are purposefully aligned with our business drivers, including:					
• Implementing the corporate strategy	2	Our selection of leadership train- ing programs have not changed over the past five years, even though our strategies and scorecard are different.	8	It raises questions about whether we are developing the future lead- ers specifically or just generically. May be better use of money if it is aimed more toward our spe- cific future needs.	HR VP; T&D manager; training vendors
• Internal orga- nizational issues and challenges, including cul- ture and cli- mate needs	7	We have added some specific topic training to address issues of diversity and sexual harassment.	8	We had to respond to these sensitive social issues . . . as much preventative as reactionary.	
Our current leadership development system is meet- ing our stra- tegic business needs.	3	Our programs and use of other devel- opment methods are old and tired. We are not being strategic. It is not adequate to address the prob- lem of many lead- ers in our company retiring in large numbers within the next **FIVE** years.	9	We do not have identified people specifically being prepared for the senior leader- ship roles. If we promote from within, we then do not have the next level ready either.	

Exhibit 2.4
Business Strategy/Need Assessment Worksheet

What business drivers and organizational needs will affect your leadership development processes? The questions and probes in this worksheet can help you forge the links between your organization's strategy and its leadership development processes. This worksheet is not all-inclusive; if you have additional questions, add them to the worksheet to complete the picture.

Regarding the format:

- Column 1 (farthest to the left) lists the questions or probes for you to consider.

- Column 2 provides a rating on a scale of 1 to 10 (1 = does not address and 10 = completely satisfied) of the degree to which your organization already does this.

- Column 3 documents the reason for your rating by providing behavioral indicators.

- Column 4 rates how important this item is on a scale of 1 to 10 (1 = not important and 10 = high importance).

- Column 5 documents your reasons for giving the importance rating you gave the probe by providing behavioral indicators.

- Column 6 (farthest to the right) identifies who should be involved to increase the rating on this item.

(Continued)

1	2	3	4	5	6
Probe/ Question	Degree Already Satisfied (1–10)	Behavioral Indicators	Degree of Importance (1–10)	Behavioral Indicators	Stakeholders
Our leadership development processes are purposefully aligned with our business drivers, including:					
• Implementing the corporate strategy					
• Internal organizational issues and challenges, including culture and climate needs					
Our current leadership development is meeting our strategic business needs:					

They are in the best position to identify the challenges associated with implementing your company's strategic plan, the pressures at play in the external environment, and the internal forces that affect your organization's performance.

Business Strategy/Organizational Needs Checklist

What is your organization's strategy for dealing with its current and future business challenges? *What is the relationship between your organization's strategy and leadership development?*

- How would you describe your organization's current strategy?

- To what degree is there a process for linking the organization's strategy and leadership development? For example, is leadership development on the agenda during the organization's planning cycle?

- Who are the key stakeholders in the strategic planning process?

- To what extent do you need their support for leadership development?

- What else is important for your organization to consider in order to make a strong link between strategy and leadership development?

Implications for Leadership

Organizations commonly announce new strategies or redefine their key business challenges. But an organization cannot move in a different direction if its approach to leadership does not change and if the organization's leaders continue to think and do the same things in the old way. This sounds obvious, but there are plenty of examples of this kind of misalignment.

Take the story of Apple Computer, for example. Before Steve Jobs returned to the helm, the company's strategy of selling Macintosh products to businesses did little to help it compete with PC-based solutions. Jobs asked the leadership of the company to re-embrace the visionary and creative flair that was the heart of the company's original vision.

Or consider the story of IBM's remarkable recovery in the 1990s. Before Lou Gerstner became CEO, IBM had lost ground to more nimble competitors because it relied too much on selling hardware and had not caught on to the idea that it was actually selling technical services and expertise. Its leadership changed its perspective on the business, and IBM regained its strength.

Many organizations struggle with issues related to mergers, acquisitions, and growth in highly competitive industries. The challenge of remaining or becoming innovative now requires a level of trust and risk taking that was previously overshadowed by conservative fiscal management. Because of an aversion to risk taking, many of the leaders in such organizations struggle to develop the competencies required to be successful in their new competitive environment.

Whenever a shift in strategy occurs, it shifts the focus of an organization's leadership. In the context of developing leadership talent, "implications for leadership" refers to the impact those shifts have on the organization's leaders. To respond effectively to new challenges, leaders must understand that what they need to do now is different from what they have done before. Consider the case of the dot-com boom in the late 1990s. Many CEOs in those dot-com organizations and other CEOs in that time adopted an entrepreneurial focus on growth. When the bubble burst, the focus shifted to survival. Strategies changed, and leadership practices changed to carry them out.

IMPLICATIONS FOR INDIVIDUALS AND ORGANIZATIONS

The leadership implications of strategic shifts are different for different parts of the organization and for individuals. With regard to the organization, a change in strategy may mean that certain functions will have to take the lead, while others must step back and collaborate more.

With regard to the individual, your organization's leaders may need to respond to the business challenges with new or significantly different behaviors, as did Apple, IBM, and Abrasive Technology. Or they may have to place greater emphasis on current behaviors. Table 3.1 is a summary of some contemporary organizational challenges and their potential implications.

The need to address emerging and different business challenges can lead to shifts of perspective and orientation that may be subtle or quite pronounced. Certainly the examples in Table 3.1 would require significant shifts for both individual leaders and the organization.

Take "expanding to international markets," for example. In that context, the senior leadership team must consider broad implications for virtually every department in the company, including structure, reporting relationships, processes, policies, and procedures.

Additionally, working internationally often requires partnerships with companies from different countries and cultures. This, in turn, requires attending to how the partner companies approach business, because it's likely to be different from how business is done domestically. For example, laws or customs in one country may not permit practices that are acceptable in another country.

The implication for leaders, especially those in senior positions, is that they must lead themselves and others in shifting perspective. Without understanding the implications of a strategic business shift, it's impossible to know which competencies may require development to prepare leaders for the change.

Table 3.1
Challenges and Their Implications for Leaders and Organizations

Organizational Challenge	Individual Leadership Implications	Organizational Leadership Implications
Expanding to international markets	More global mind-set, broader systems thinking, increased understanding of cross-cultural leadership	The new strategy reorganizes units into product groups that span countries
Shifting from a product-focused to a solutions-focused business	Increased cross-functional collaboration replaces protected expertise	Developing customer-intimate processes
Shifting from a pre-merger mind-set to a post-merger mind-set	Greater individual authority, responsibility, and risk taking	Shifting from top-down leadership to more empowerment and moving decision making to the lowest appropriate level
Need for increased innovation, especially in the use and application of technology to meet evolving market demands	Comfort with change; adaptability and flexibility	Processes, policies, and procedures that allow and enable individuals to experiment and take risks
Developing talent to meet future organization leadership needs	Increased emphasis on performance-based feedback, coaching skills, and other developmental activities	Shifting the responsibility for development to line managers instead of viewing it as an HR responsibility

As you consider the leadership implications of your organization's strategy, you can begin to prioritize development needs. Some challenges may require more urgent responses than others. Some are short-term (increase or decrease sales staff, for example), and some are long-term responses (building and leading virtual, international work teams or selling off assets, for example).

IDENTIFYING LEADERSHIP IMPLICATIONS

To begin exploring leadership implications, ask yourself questions such as:

- What action would you expect your leaders to take in response to these challenges?
- What actions would you expect your leaders to do more of or less of?
- What happens if your organization's leaders do not make these changes?

Record your conclusions on the Leadership Implications Worksheet (Exhibit 3.1), and then ask others (key executives and representative constituent groups) for their thoughts to add to your perspective. The worksheet includes additional prompts and probes to help you explore the leadership implications of current and future organizational strategy. The tool does not cover every instance, and you are certain to think of similar prompts you can use in your specific context. Here are some examples of modifications that some of our clients have made:

1. Questions related to a product recall and the potential impact it had on the company's public image.
2. Questions related to public safety after an explosion at one of its manufacturing plants.
3. Questions related to corporate social responsibility as it related to environmental impact and going green.
4. Questions related to consumer privacy.
5. Questions related to increased public scrutiny of accounting practices.

A final word: The forms here are not what's important. The important thing is to gather the data and think through what it means. People responsible for developing leadership talent in their organizations often undervalue or skip over the important step of identifying the leadership implications of current and expected business challenges. This may occur because the process of identifying implications requires some exploration, which may feel uncomfortably ambiguous when the organization is demanding action and results. Nevertheless, the consequence of moving too quickly through this step is that important things may be overlooked and resources may be unnecessarily spent.

Exhibit 3.1
Leadership Implications Worksheet

What business challenges and strategic shifts will affect your leadership development processes? What actions would you expect your leaders to take in response to these challenges? What actions would you expect your leaders to do more of or less of? What happens if your organization's leaders do not make these changes?

The questions and probes in this worksheet can help you connect the implications of your organization's strategic challenges and its leadership development processes. This worksheet is not all-inclusive; if you have additional questions, add them to the worksheet to complete the picture.

As in similar worksheets:

- Column 1 (farthest to the left) lists the questions or probes for you to consider.

- Column 2 provides a rating on a scale of 1 to 10 (1 = does not address and 10 = completely satisfied) of the degree to which your organization already does this.

- Column 3 documents the reason for your rating by providing behavioral indicators.

- Column 4 rates how important this item is on a scale of 1 to 10 (1 = not important and 10 = high importance).

- Column 5 documents your reasons for giving the importance rating you gave the probe by providing behavioral indicators.

- Column 6 (farthest to the right) identifies who should be involved to increase the rating on this item.

(Continued)

1	2	3	4	5	6
Probe/ Question	Degree Already Satisfied (1–10)	Behavioral Indicators	Degree of Importance (1–10)	Behavioral Indicators	Stake-holders
We know what leadership actions must be emphasized:					
• To implement corporate strategy					
• To address competitive and market-place issues					
• To resolve internal orga-nizational issues					
We know how this emphasis differs from what was asked in the past.					
Our leaders make them-selves available to identify and discuss the actions that are needed to achieve our goals.					
Our leaders demonstrate how these actions differ from what was asked of them in the past.					
Other:					

Implications for Leadership Checklist

What must be different or change in some way (including the mind-set of leaders as well as business processes) to ensure that your organization achieves its strategy? *What must the organization's leaders be able to do differently in order to implement its strategy? What organizational capabilities must be different—and how do they have to be different (e.g., increasing skills in one area and/or decreasing emphasis in another).*

- How will your organization's leaders need to think and act differently in order to support the organization's strategy?

- What will key functions or departments within your organization need to do differently? How does this impact what your leaders will need to do differently?

- What has your organization already done to address leadership development?

- What development will your organization's leaders require to support the strategy?

- Traditionally, how has your organization demonstrated commitment to leadership development?

- What new or additional organizational commitment and support are now required?

Leadership Competencies

After surveying your organization's strategy, identifying the challenges to implementing it, and exploring their leadership implications, you can start to identify a coherent set of leadership competencies. These skills describe in behavioral terms what your leaders will need to do to address those challenges. As with the other parts of the DLT approach, there are organizational and individual levels to competencies. This chapter focuses on competencies for individual leader development. Keep in mind that individual competencies are most meaningful and have the most impact when they are aligned with the organization's strategic context.

Consider also what core competencies the organization needs to develop or emphasize in order to address its challenges and how that development extends to various organizational functions. For example, when IBM shifted to a service orientation—an organization selling solutions—individuals certainly needed to change their behavior. But the units they worked in also had to change the way they operated—and sometimes what they did.

Or recall when Xerox was teetering on the brink of bankruptcy; its leadership had to communicate a sense of urgency while at the same time re-engaging employees who were already tired and disenchanted. The challenge Xerox faced was in finding leaders who could balance multiple competing needs: being optimistic and at the same time being realistic about the difficulties the company was facing. Another competing need Xerox leaders had to address at the same time was the importance of making tough business decisions while being empathetic to the workforce.

One last example: When the CEO of Abrasive Technology, a manufacturer of diamond grinding tools, made the bold decision to shift to a process-centered structure to keep its growth momentum strong, its leadership team had to learn to operate at higher levels of effectiveness. A new model of leadership, production, and service was required, one that did not look anything like the contemporary corporate mind-set.

The set of competencies you identify can bring focus to the leadership capacities that are most important for your organization. When expressed in behavioral terms (see Exhibit 4.1), competencies create common criteria and therefore a common language with which to view behavior. That makes it easier to give and receive feedback about performance. Further, competencies are a core integrating element of talent management in general, and can be used for selection and development across the organization (American Productivity and Quality Center, 2004).

A LEADERSHIP COMPETENCY MODEL

Without a competency model, it can be difficult to provide organizational consistency in reinforcing specific leadership behavior. It also can be difficult to establish alignment of individual leadership behavior with organizational strategy.

Your organization may already have a competency model in place. Even so, it's useful to periodically reexamine that model in light of emerging challenges. Your organization may want or need to shift the emphasis from some competencies to others.

For example, imagine you work in a biotech company. Since the company's founding, its focus has been almost entirely on research. Recently, the research has proved successful and the company must now shift its focus to producing and marketing its breakout product. That shift brings with it different strategic organizational challenges, which may have to be answered with a different set of leadership competencies.

In other cases, a turnaround or restructuring, for example, it may be worthwhile to establish a new set of leadership competencies to supplant most of the existing ones. Deciding to create a new model depends on the degree of difference between the organization's old way of working and what is necessary for success in the future.

The point is, competencies and competency models are not static. They must be reexamined periodically and updated as needed. We recommend a formal review every few years or whenever the organization experiences a significant change, such as a plant closing or merger.

Exhibit 4.1
The Behavioral Language of Competencies

When competencies are written in behavioral terms, they facilitate development. Here are two examples of behavioral descriptions:

- Identifies and removes barriers to effective teamwork
- Maintains smooth, effective working relationships

That is, does the statement of competency describe a "behavior" that can be observed? The difference is between generalities and specifics. Here are a couple of examples:

General	Descriptive Behavior
Confronting problem employees	Can deal effectively with resistant employees. Acts decisively when faced with a tough decision such as laying off workers. Is able to fire or deal firmly with loyal but incompetent people without procrastinating.
Building and mending relationships with others	Gets things done without creating unnecessary adversarial relationships. Tries to understand what other people think before making judgments about them.

These descriptions improve the ability to see both the presence and absence of those behaviors. Without a guiding set of competencies that everyone in the organization can agree on, leaders operate from their own perspectives or definitions about what is acceptable behavior.

Here are some guidelines to take into consideration as possible drivers for reviewing your organization's leadership competencies:

1. A significant shift in your organization's strategy

2. Changes in the competitive landscape

3. A breakthrough in technology that impacts your business

4. Changes in government regulations that impact your business

CHOOSING YOUR MODEL

There are several well-established lists of leadership competencies in the leadership development market (see Appendix A for CCL's complete leadership competency list; also see the Recommended Resources in this book). Among those, there is significant overlap. In reviewing different models, it's best to adopt leadership competencies that have been researched and validated. Such research creates a congruent set of underlying behaviors that, when viewed as a whole, reflect established, effective leadership practices. For example, CCL has collected thousands of responses from leaders in all kinds of organizations as to what the most critical competencies are in their organizations. Table 4.1 shows how often organizations select specific competencies when customizing CCL's competency list.

Table 4.1 CCL Competencies: Frequency of Use in Customized 360-Degree Feedback Assessments		
1	Leading Employees	57%
2	Building and Mending Relationships	54%
3	Change Management	52%
4	Risk Taking, Innovation	52%
5	Influencing, Leadership, Power	50%
6	Communicating Information, Ideas	40%
7	Taking Action, Making Decisions, Following Through	38%
8	Brings Out the Best in People	38%
9	Listening	35%
10	Openness to Influence; Flexibility	34%

Beware of competencies that lack the statistical rigor of good research. Popular trends and compelling labels can be misleading. You cannot construct an effective competency model by making up behaviors that you think might be helpful or that you think your organization might find interesting.

CCL'S COLLECTION OF LEADER COMPETENCIES

Each of the items on CCL's competency wheel (see Figure 4.1) is statistically valid and reliable. CCL organizes its competency collection from very general

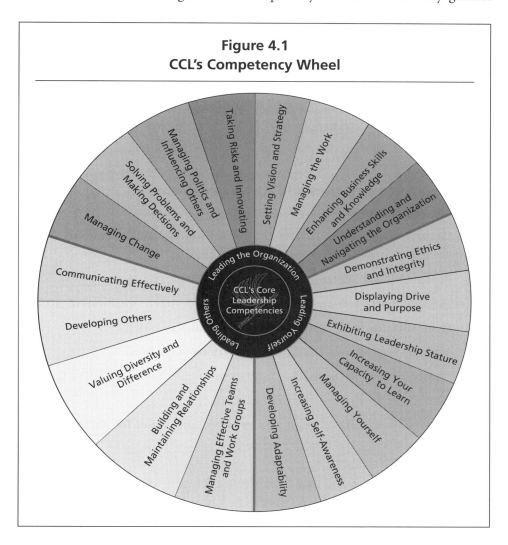

**Figure 4.1
CCL's Competency Wheel**

elements associated with leadership, to clusters of related competencies, to yet more specific elements (competencies), and finally to specific behaviors.

Notice that the hub of CCL's wheel is divided into three categories: Leading Yourself, Leading Others, and Leading the Organization. The three categories divide into twenty competency clusters. Each of these competency clusters consists of specific competencies and behaviors that describe them. (See Appendix A for a more complete list of competencies and behaviors revealed and confirmed by CCL's research.)

DEVELOPING A COMPETENCY MODEL

The process described in this section uses CCL's wheel, but it can be adapted to a model of your own design. To make the description of the process more accessible, we will use a running example that focuses on teamwork competencies (see the following listing). The competencies you select for your organization's model should align with its strategy and challenges, and with the leader behaviors you have identified as crucial to carrying out that strategy and meeting those challenges.

Examples of Competencies and Associated Behaviors

Leading the Organization

Managing Change: These leaders can demonstrate an understanding of the impact that change can have on individuals' lives.

- Recognizes and names personal feelings
- Demonstrates openness to sharing his or her feelings in situations of change
- Demonstrates a willingness to hear the feelings of others
- Manages his/her own emotions in situations of change
- Resists the urge to fix people's feelings or to talk them out of their feelings
- Respects and welcomes the feelings of others
- Shows appreciation of feelings as an important part of the change process

Leading Others

Managing Effective Teams and Work Groups: These leaders have a talent with people that is evident in their ability to pull people together into highly effective teams.

- Is able to pull people together around a common goal
- Is able to bring out the best in people
- Can turn a group into a high-performing team
- Is able to achieve consensus even when people disagree on the best course of action
- Has a special talent for dealing with people
- Works with and utilizes teams in a manner that enhances their effectiveness
- Utilizes groups in problem-solving tasks
- Negotiates adeptly with individuals and groups regarding roles and/or resources
- When working with team members, facilitates a climate of cooperation and collaboration
- Builds an effective team

Leading Yourself

Developing Adaptability: These leaders understand their own impact on situations and people; they accurately sense when to give and take.

- Tailors communication based on others' needs, motivations, and agendas
- Influences others without using formal authority
- Knows when and with whom to build alliances
- Wins concessions from others without harming relationships
- Adjusts leadership style according to the demands of the situation
- Accurately senses when to give and take when negotiating

Step 1. Assume, for example, that your organization's strategy implies a much greater need for effective teamwork. Leaders will need to work more collaboratively in their own units and across functions. Project teams will have to form quickly and adjourn at the close of a project.

Step 2. Because teams involve working with others, it is logical to look to the Leading Others category for those competencies associated with teamwork.

Step 3. Within the Leading Others category, there are several potential clusters to consider. In keeping with this example, you select the cluster of Managing Effective Teams and Work Groups.

Step 4. Within that cluster, there are several related competencies to consider. For illustration purposes, consider the idea that your organization's leaders will have to encourage and motivate their teams to achieve the company's strategic aims. With that in mind, you select the competency, Brings Out the Best in People.

Step 5. The behaviors associated with that competency are listed below. These are the behaviors leaders in your organization should develop. With these clear guidelines, others in the organization can provide developmental feedback, and developing leaders have a benchmark against which to measure their progress.

Behaviors Associated with Bringing Out the Best in People

- Is able to pull people together around a common goal
- Can turn a group into a high-performing team
- Is able to achieve consensus even when people disagree on the best course of action
- Has a special talent for dealing with people

INVOLVE OTHERS

Examining the behaviors that define a competency is important but difficult work. For that reason, it's best not to leave the task of developing a competency model to a small group of people in your organization, such as the HR department or a special committee of executives. During the competency model development phase, it's valuable to gather the input of line managers, senior leaders, and other stakeholders.

To minimize the inherent biases of small groups, the different perspectives of all stakeholders are important. Clarity about the required skills and behaviors informs the organization about what specific development is necessary to ensure future success. Use the Stakeholder Identification Worksheet (Exhibit 4.2) to identify stakeholders who can help you develop a competency model that makes sense for your organization.

A final word: A sound, well-thought-out competency model is useless unless it is integrated into the fabric of the organization. For example, your set of competencies can be crafted into a 360-degree feedback tool; performance management plans can focus on the related behaviors; and compensation plans can be aligned with the organization's leadership competency model. In the best circumstances,

Exhibit 4.2
Stakeholder Identification Worksheet

List and describe the stakeholders in the organization who are involved in the leadership development initiative or have an interest in its outcome. Do not just look at the top people in the organization. Include the designers of the initiative, trainers, human resources staff, potential participants, senior managers concerned with the results, managers whose staff will participate in the initiative, and the groups funding the initiative.

This list of questions isn't exhaustive, but offers guidance. If your circumstances suggest other questions, substitute them for these, or add them to this list.

	Name	Stakeholder Position and/or Description	Stakeholder Interest
Who has an interest in the development initiative?			
Who has an interest in the evaluation's processes and results?			
Are there additional people whose support is required for the success of the initiative or the evaluation?			
Who has decision-making authority with respect to both the initiative and the evaluation?			
Other:			

all talent management processes complement the competencies you describe for developing leadership talent.

Leadership Competencies Checklist

What knowledge and skills do your organization's leaders need to address the implications of its strategy? *What competencies must be developed? What organizational capabilities?*

- How will you determine what competencies your leaders need?

- What new leader competencies do you anticipate needing to develop in order to support your organization's strategy?

- What existing leader competencies are critical to maintain or improve?

- Is there a prioritized order for developing these leader competencies? If so, what is it?

- Do you need to differentiate these competencies based on the leader's organizational level?

- Will development of these competencies build necessary organizational capability? How?

Gaps, Skills, and Target Populations

By following the DLT approach so far, at this point you have identified the business and strategic challenges facing your organization, you have taken into account the leadership implications, and you have matched that information to a set of competencies needed to address the challenges. Your next step is to determine to what extent development is required.

This chapter focuses on three areas: (1) gap analysis (what competencies need development); (2) level of skill development (how skilled in a particular competency leaders should be); and (3) target population (candidates for development).

FUNDAMENTALS OF GAP ANALYSIS

The term *gap analysis* refers to a comparison between a current state and a desired state. In the context of developing leadership talent, the purpose of a gap analysis is to determine your organization's and its leadership's performance against the set of competencies that you have developed or verified. A DLT gap analysis (see Figure 5.1) examines the current state (determine the skills, knowledge, and abilities of your organization and its leaders) and the desired or future state (identify the necessary conditions for organizational and individual leader success).

The difference between the current state and the future state defines the gap that must be closed through some type of leader or leadership development process.

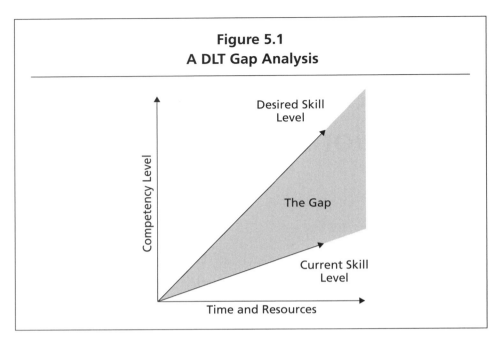

Figure 5.1
A DLT Gap Analysis

Desired Skill
Level

Competency Level

The Gap

Current Skill
Level

Time and Resources

Defining the Current State

There are several methods to use to collect information about the current state of leadership within your organization. It's best to use multiple methods for collecting data in order to form a complete picture. Information sources include:

- Data from climate surveys or employee opinion surveys
- Targeted surveys
- Aggregated data from individual 360-degree questionnaires
- Interviews with members of the target population
- Consultation with individuals in key positions and/or with specific knowledge of your organization's leadership
- Direct observation of individual members of the target population
- Employee and management focus groups

While gathering data, you might find it helpful to use specific prompts and probes designed to elicit informative responses. For example, we rely on the structure in CCL's Leadership Competency Profile Tool, which gathers information about perceived levels of skill and organizational importance on specific competencies (see Figure 5.2). It is an example of a targeted survey and is based

Figure 5.2
Sample Leadership Competency Profile

Number of Respondents: 6

Competency Area	Importance	Skill	Difference	
Leading Others — Maintaining Effective Teams and Work Groups	5.83	4.50	−1.33	−
Building and Maintaining Relationships	5.67	4.83	−0.83	
Valuing Diversity and Difference	4.83	5.00	0.17	
Developing Others	5.00	5.00	0.00	
Communicating Effectively	6.00	5.00	−1.00	
Leading the Organization — Managing Change	6.17	5.17	−1.00	
Solving Problems and Making Decisions	5.50	5.50	0.00	
Managing Politics and Influencing Others	5.00	5.00	0.00	
Taking Risks and Innovating	4.33	4.17	−0.17	
Setting Vision and Strategy	5.33	4.33	−1.00	
Managing the Work	5.17	5.33	0.17	
Enhancing Business Skills and Knowledge	4.83	5.00	0.17	
Understanding and Navigating the Organization	5.83	5.00	−0.83	
Leading Yourself — Demonstrating Ethics and Integrity	6.17	6.83	0.67	
Displaying Drive and Purpose	4.50	6.00	1.50	+
Exhibiting Leadership Stature	4.33	4.83	0.50	
Increasing Your Capacity to Learn	4.50	4.33	−0.17	
Managing Yourself	5.17	5.00	−0.17	
Increasing Self-Awareness	5.00	4.67	−0.33	
Developing Adaptability	5.00	4.83	−0.17	

Legend:
Difference = Skill − Importance
+/− = The difference is 1.00 or more ("+" = Skill is higher; "−" = Skill is lower)
Rating Definitions:
1 = Not Important; 3 = Somewhat Important; 5 = Important; 7 = Critically Important

upon CCL's Typology of Leader Competencies. See Appendix B for a copy of the complete tool.

Defining the Future State

By identifying the business challenges facing the organization's strategy, implications for leaders and leadership, and constructing your company's competency model, you have already made steps toward defining the future state. All of the data-gathering mechanisms that were listed for defining the current state are applicable here as well. For example, in addition to the Leadership Competency Profile Tool, we often use some of the questions on the Interview Guide presented in Chapter 2 (Exhibit 2.1).

Other information for determining the desired future state of your organization include

- Business and strategic plans
- Vision and mission statements
- SWOT (strengths-weaknesses-opportunities-threats) documents
- Financial targets and performance indicators/reports
- Short- and long-term goal statements
- Balanced scorecard
- "Dashboard" metric indicators

To fill out the picture of the desired or necessary conditions for organizational and individual leader success in leading the business, add relevant questions or probes to your data gathering (interviews, observation, focus groups, and the like). For example, the head of learning and development for a global manufacturing company interviewed all the members of the executive team, asking them what the ideal future state looked like in terms of leadership skills. He then compared and contrasted this information with data he had collected from 360-degree feedback tools to identify both the current and desired future states.

At some point in the process, you might find it helpful to assess what tools are currently in place to help identify gaps. Use the Gaps, Skills, and Target Populations Worksheet (Exhibit 5.1) as a guide. In the responses that use a 1 to 10 scale, 1 refers to the least degree, and 10 refers to the highest degree.

Exhibit 5.1

Gaps, Skills, and Target Populations Worksheet

Probe/Question	Degree Already Satisfied (1–10)	Behavioral Indicators	Degree of Importance (1–10)	Behavioral Indicators	Stakeholders
We have systematic methods for gathering information about current leadership effectiveness. • Performance Reviews • Talent Reviews/Audits • Aggregated 360 data • Other					
We can demonstrate that closing the identified gaps will contribute to leadership effectiveness.					
There is a system in place for identifying candidates for leadership development initiatives. • In anticipation of promotion? • High-potential candidate(s)? • In response to a developmental problem for an individual? • As reward for good performance? • To maintain or build knowledge and skills?					
Other:					

LEVEL OF SKILL DEVELOPMENT

Think of levels of learning and performance (see Figure 5.3) as how long it will take members of the target population to achieve some level of knowledge, skill proficiency as a result of the development initiative, or organizational change. Each level provides a platform for further development to the next level. It is our belief that learning and performance are linked. The use of the terms together is intentional because learning is enhanced by application, and because performance is improved by learning. As the complexity for learning increases, the time required for acquiring the learning also increases. For example, how long will it take a leader to develop effective coaching skills? The first step toward an answer is to increase the leader's awareness of why it is important to coach his or her direct reports (to support their personal and professional development). A leader could develop that awareness within a few hours (or less). If you want more skilled coaching leaders, it will take more time and practice. Or, if you want to take that coaching capability to the next level and develop organizational capacity, then it will take significantly more planning, time, and effort.

Some factors that determine the specific length of time necessary to achieve each level of learning and performance include individual or group abilities and

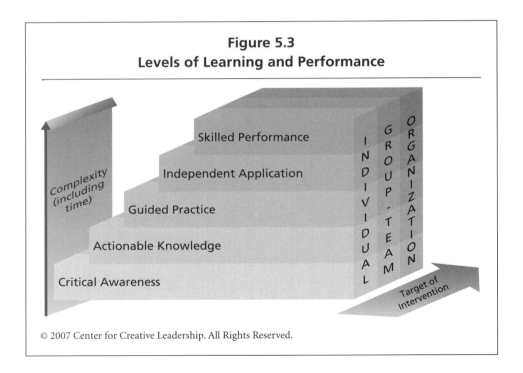

Figure 5.3
Levels of Learning and Performance

motivation, organizational commitment to leadership development, and access to high-quality leadership development resources. When individuals and groups are functioning at the independent application level, real behavior change has occurred. Performance and learning peak at the skilled performance level, when new behaviors are integrated into the leader's practice.

Some caution should be exercised at this point. When you define a level of learning and performance for your target population, do not use it just to help your organization understand what resources will be required in order to reach the desired skill level. This is also the time to begin thinking about what methods you will use both to reach the next stage and to evaluate the outcomes of your development initiative (see Chapter 8). Paying attention to these three details will help ensure that the results are in line with your stakeholders' expectations. A stakeholder who expects to reach skilled performance levels after a three-day development program will be disappointed.

IDENTIFYING TARGET POPULATIONS

The challenge in many organizations is that there are too many employees to be targeted for purposeful development. There is no simple answer about whom to target because the choice depends on the strategic direction of the company, the business challenges it faces, and its anticipated needs for future leadership talent. In other words, decisions about how to focus development should be driven by the organization's business needs and what the leadership pipeline requires.

Decisions about whom to develop may be based on either broad or specific goals. For example, a broad goal might involve emphasizing the needs of high-potential leaders. An example of a specific goal might be to develop a skill set in sales leaders so that they can coach and guide sales representatives.

For our purposes, the discussion here focuses on three common target populations: new hires, high potentials, and solid performers.

New Hires

As a target population for development, new hires present several different opportunities. One occurs when employees join the organization. This is the opportunity to introduce new hires to the organization's culture and its leadership competency model. Another opportunity for development of new hires is when the organization is intentionally trying to shift its culture as a strategic initiative. New hires also present an opportunity to further assess their potential to be future leaders. It is more effective to teach new hires the desired set of competencies at the start of their tenure than it is to let their previous practices prevail or allow your organization's current culture to influence their behavior, which then has to be undone and relearned.

High Potentials

High potentials are frequently the targets of leadership development efforts. In the book *Grow Your Own Leaders: How to Identify, Develop, and Retain Leadership Talent*, Byham, Smith, and Paese (2002) define high-potential employees as able to advance at least two or three levels, "those who will yield the highest return on the company's investment in development resources" (p. 61).

Another way to define this group is as employees who demonstrate the ability to learn. They have the potential to take advantage and learn from experience. High potentials typically consider learning as a value in and of itself and are driven to learn as a goal.

But although some high-potential candidates are smart, aggressive, and can exceed their performance measures, they can be missing the emotional competencies necessary for senior-level leadership, according to a *Harvard Business Review* article titled "The Young and the Clueless" (Bunker, Kram, & Ting, 2002). It's important to develop those competencies before or as part of a promotion. At some point, a manager's raw talent and determined ambition become less important than the ability to influence and persuade.

How do you identify a high potential? You could use an assessment battery or assessment center. Alternatively, you could base your assessment of potential on observation of on-the-job performance. Research tells us that there are observable indicators of high potential. Lominger suggests that we should attend to indicators of learning agility, of which there are four types: people agility, results agility, mental agility, and change agility (Lombardo & Eichinger, 2002). The Corporate Leadership Council (2001) has a complementary list. They say we should attend to ability, aspiration, and engagement. As we said before, high performance in one job is not a guarantee of high performance at a higher level—especially if that job is in another function. Nevertheless, performance is where you start. Whatever else you do, observation of on-the-job performance is an essential element.

Solid Performers

In the rush to identify and develop new hires and high potentials, some organizations discount the solid performers. However, every organization needs such people in order to keep its baseline functions running smoothly. Solid performers may be individual contributors or department or functional heads who, for either organizational or personal reasons, are not destined to become senior-level executives. An important distinction to keep in mind here is that, while every high potential is also a solid performer, not every solid performer is a high potential. Also, even when a solid performer may be a high-potential candidate, he or she may not aspire to an executive-level position.

The focus of development for solid performers should recognize and manage their abilities for the benefit of the organization. Typically, the skills to be developed are in the areas of individual contributions, being able to separate the important contributions from the mundane, and harnessing their strengths to achieve the goals of specific organizational departments or areas.

A final word: It is said that you cannot know where you are going unless you know where you have been. In the same way, you cannot know where you are going unless you have an idea of where you want to go. We hope that the gap analysis work in this chapter has helped you find an answer to those questions by outlining tactics for gathering information and suggesting a path for helping your organization reach its desired state of leadership development.

A gap analysis is but one part of the answer. To prepare your organization for the work of developing leadership talent, you also must figure out what level of leadership skill is needed and how long it might take to develop competencies so that leaders can put them into practice with confidence. Further, you must define your DLT efforts for different populations in your organization. New hires have to come up to speed; high potentials need development to take on greater leadership roles; and solid performers must have a developmental path that encourages them to stay with the organization and build its bench strength. With this groundwork in place, you are ready to implement specific development strategies to help your organization move from its current state to the future state it envisions, and which it requires to sustain its success.

Gaps, Skills, and Target Populations Checklist

What is the difference between the current state of your target population and the desired state in the context of the competencies you have identified? *Who will be developed (individuals or groups), and what is their current skill level compared to the needed level?*

- Are there target functions and/or departments for your leadership development process? If so, what are they?

- What are the target populations for your leader-development process? Do they come from the above functions and departments? Will focusing on these populations build capability?

- How should you prioritize the development of those populations?

- Does a competency or skill gap exist for these target populations?

- What is the gap between the current competencies and future desired and needed competencies?

- To what level of proficiency do these competencies have to be developed? Does this vary from one target population to another?

Development Strategies

At this point in the DLT approach, you have done some form of gap analysis to identify the difference between the current state of development and the desired state. Now you start building your plan.

This chapter describes ways to close the gaps you identified by exploring some of the strategies that you can use to develop your organization's leadership talent. First, we review some of the core principles CCL takes into consideration when designing a leadership development initiative. Second, we discuss specific strategies that you can use in developing your organization's leaders.

The principles and strategies outlined in this chapter do not form a simple checklist of activities or behaviors that generate effective leaders. If there is one key idea in the DLT approach, it is that leadership development is *an ongoing process* that is never complete. Learning and change happen slowly, over the course of a career, during which one experience is linked to another as part of a larger, continuous process.

PRINCIPLES OF DEVELOPMENT

People learn from their experiences. Research and practice show there are three key elements that make the difference between an average experience and one that drives leader development: assessment, challenge, and support (see Chapter 1 for a complete discussion). As you are responsible for developing leadership talent in your organization, designing a development strategy around experiences that combine these elements is more likely to bring about the results your organization needs. In addition to the elements of assessment, challenge, and support, there are other important development principles that help people learn from their experiences: learning to learn, variety of experiences, and emotional intelligence.

Learning to Learn

Learning takes place on multiple levels: cognitive (more information), behavioral (do things differently), and emotional (feelings are always present and they influence perceptions and choices). Given that learning involves all of those domains, CCL uses the phrase "learning to learn" because we believe it is useful for leaders to examine how they learn so that they can enhance what they learn.

CCL research identifies four common clusters of learning tactics that adults use when confronting new or ambiguous challenges: thinking, taking action, accessing others, and feelings (Dalton, 1998). The research suggests that a more versatile learner (one who uses more than one tactic to address a challenge) is more effective at learning from experience than someone who applies only a favored, single tactic.

In linking this to developing leadership talent, it is compelling to consider that continuous learning is an antidote for the most common derailment factor: inability to adapt to change. Nobody would say that leaders are not smart. But they can limit their development if they rely on just one or two learning tactics. Like the rest of us, leaders often fall into patterns of thinking or acting that are useful to solving problems, but then a new situation arises and they find that they are overly dependent on those patterns. Encourage the leaders in your organization to examine how they learn by having them reflect on their learning experiences. This practice can enhance their learning skills and motivate them to continue learning.

For example, it can be useful for people to have a model of learning in mind. Such mental models can help people make sense of the sensations that accompany learning experiences. Many otherwise effective learning initiatives have gone astray because people misinterpreted how they experience the learning process. Profound learning often brings with it a mix of feelings. Some of those feeling are pleasant (a sense of accomplishment or personal growth, for example), and some of those feelings are not so pleasant (doubt, for example, or a concern about performance).

If you can help leaders in your organization to remain steady on their development paths, to continue applying the lessons they learn even if they experience the discomfort of doubt, then those leaders can make a profound difference in their choice of effective actions. This is where the support part of CCL's ACS model becomes so critical. People naturally pursue equilibrium when knocked off balance, usually by retreating to what has worked for them in the past. It takes a focused (and supported) effort to tolerate ambiguity while growing more comfortable with new skills and perceptions. When managers understand these normal reactions to new learning, they can often circumvent that natural tendency. They can also learn to generate support of their own, which goes a long way in creating a learning-oriented climate.

Variety of Experiences

Preferred learning tactics, psychological preferences, and educational experiences all influence how people learn. Some people learn best from reading information, others learn better from experiential activities, and others need repeated exposures in different settings. Because each person is different, it is difficult to predict precisely the level of learning from any particular experience (Van Velsor, Moxley, & Bunker, 2004). It seems obvious that a variety of tactics are necessary to effectively transmit skills and information to a group or to an entire level of managers in a company. But far too many development initiatives limit themselves.

Historically, training has meant classroom-based events. But computer-based learning and online programs have grown in popularity. Coaching to support learning is also a tactic gaining favor. CCL research shows that, although important, methods such as these make up less than 20 percent of the key learning events in a manager's career. The most important sources of learning come from challenging assignments and hardships. In short, managers gain their most profound learning from live experience. Classroom events, coaching support, and other sources of learning must be geared toward a real-world setting.

Adults pursue learning in areas that serve them, and the value of learning must exceed the cost and effort required to gain it. The successful integration of new skills comes when managers are able to apply a variety of experiences to their work.

Emotional Intelligence

Another important principle to consider in designing a leadership development process is emotional intelligence. Important research in this area has been going on for many years. Daniel Goleman popularized the phrase in his book *Emotional Intelligence: Why It Can Matter More Than IQ* (1995), and other writers and researchers have also investigated the concept. The various models of emotional intelligence competencies can be clustered in four groups: self-awareness, self-management, social awareness, and social skills.

Self-awareness involves understanding motives and feelings that influence perception and decisions. Self-management refers to choosing the most effective action in a situation. Social awareness requires an accurate assessment of others and their likely reactions. Social skills call for an authentic and integrity-driven interaction with others.

Advances in neuroscience have shown that individuals are born with a certain amount of emotional intelligence, and recent studies clearly indicate that these competencies can be developed with regular practice and feedback (Cherniss & Adler, 2000). This development requires self-awareness, the motivation to learn about oneself, support and encouragement from others, repeated practice over time, and regular developmental feedback.

Studies by CCL show that the primary causes of derailment in executives involve deficits in emotional intelligence competencies. Inability to adapt to change, and difficulties in effectively managing relationships—the two most common derailment indicators—are both grounded in poor emotional intelligence competence. There is compelling evidence that emotional intelligence has a direct effect on leadership effectiveness.

At CCL, we take these issues into consideration by following a number of core principles for designing leadership development programs, listed below:

Key Principles in the DLT Approach

- Leader development and personal development are interdependent and lifelong.
- Leader development best occurs in an environment rich in ongoing assessment, challenge, and support.
- Leader development cannot take place without the ability to learn. This ability is acquired and strengthened through sustained and disciplined activities and behaviors.
- Leaders learn from a variety of sources; for example, challenging jobs (stretch assignments, turnaround projects), other people (coaches, mentors, significant

others in one's life), hardships (loss of job, demotion, missed promotion), and certain other experiences (development programs, further education, volunteer work, parenting). The leadership development process should be closely linked to and support the strategic plan of the organization.

- Organizations should have updated success profiles that identify the leader competencies most critical to meet their current and anticipated business challenges.

- Assessment for development is different in purpose and application from assessment for selection or appraisal.

- Assessment-for-development processes involve an individual's assessment of strengths and weaknesses, identification and articulation of the goals one wants to reach, formulating a viable strategy for development, and implementing the strategy with a mix of ongoing challenge, feedback, and support.

- The responsibility for development rests primarily with the individual; however, development may take place more effectively and quickly when supported by the individual's manager and the organization.

- Derailment is most likely when there is an inability to learn.

- Job assignments are most developmental when they have certain kinds of challenges embedded in them.

- The impact of leadership development initiatives can and should be measured.

Keep in mind also that people learn from similar experiences but in different ways and to differing degrees. Because each person is different, it is difficult to predict precisely the level of learning from any particular experience (Van Velsor, Moxley, & Bunker, 2004). Leaders often learn how to direct and motivate others in early supervisory experiences, they tend to learn about organizational and management values from their bosses, and they often learn how to deal with stress from a business mistake. New types of experiences can expand their repertoire of leadership skills.

Whether your development focus is the individual or a group of varying sizes, CCL's research and experience show that such development is enhanced by using assessment, challenge, and support. In fact, you can make any experience—a training program, an assignment, a relationship—richer and more developmental by ensuring that these three elements are part of the design. Exhibit 6.1 shows

Exhibit 6.1
Sample Individual Development Planning Worksheet

Strategies	Assessment	Challenge	Support	Notes
Challenging Job Assignment				
Learning from Others • Role Models • Mentor(s) • Coaches • Networks				
Ongoing Feedback				
Training and Reading				
Other:				

What is your goal in developing this person? What is the purpose for development?

one way to incorporate this thinking into an individual development worksheet; the same format could be used to outline a plan for a target group.

Effective and measurable leadership development is not just a matter of exposing individuals to a series of experiences or opportunities for learning. Organizational context plays a role as well. Any leader-development process is embedded in a particular environment, which includes the organization's business strategy, its culture, and its systems and processes. This context shapes the leader-development process and its focus.

Consider your own organization. There undoubtedly are certain types of expertise and experience that are essential for someone to rise in its ranks. It is important to know what those are and the types of developmental experiences (assignments as well as classroom work) that can help your organization build the leadership it needs.

BUILDING DEVELOPMENTAL EXPERIENCES

At this point in the DLT process, you know the details of what has to be developed in your target populations. Now it is time to build the appropriate developmental experiences.

A wide range of strategies are available for creating developmental experiences. Here we will describe four that CCL research and experience show to be most relevant for developing leadership talent: developmental job assignments, developmental relationships, structured development programs, and 360-degree and personality assessment questionnaires. Each of these strategies is discussed individually, but we recommend they be used in various combinations.

DEVELOPMENTAL JOB ASSIGNMENTS

Training workshops, business classes, and other classroom-related development opportunities are helpful, but it is experience that provides the greatest opportunity for developing leadership talent. CCL's expansive research and extensive experience in this area shows that:

- People learn best from practical experience on and off the job.

- Effective leaders continue to develop their skills and to expand the variety of those skills throughout their careers.

- The greater the variety of experiences, the greater the likelihood of developing a broad range of skills.

This means that developmental job assignments are more likely to contribute the most to individual leader development. Sometimes, these assignments can be promotions, but often these are assignments for development in place (developing while working the same job or role). Also, in keeping with the principle that development is often up to the individual, leaders in your organization do not have to wait for an assignment. They can choose their own developmental experiences.

What makes a job or task developmental is that it stretches you, pushes you out of your comfort zone, and requires you to think and act beyond what you might have thought possible. Here's an example: A high-technology company identified Michael as a high-potential employee for a general manager position. Michael is a certified public accountant with experience in finance. However, his background has left him with too narrow a functional orientation. In order to provide Michael with broader experience, his organization scheduled him for several different job rotation assignments, including time spent in Human Resources, Marketing, and Customer Service (see Exhibit 6.2). These rotations will better prepare Michael for a general manager role, which is what this company needs and it is consistent with Michael's aspirations.

Developmental assignments often put people in situations in which they have to solve problems, overcome obstacles, and make risky choices. To help you identify possibilities for developmental assignments, check the following list of ten key job challenges that stimulate learning.

Ten Key Job Challenges That Stimulate Learning

1. Unfamiliar responsibilities—handling responsibilities that are new or very different from previous ones

2. New directions—starting something new or making strategic changes

3. Inherited problems—fixing problems created by someone else or that existed before taking the assignment

4. Problems with employees—dealing with employees who lack adequate experience, are incompetent, or are resistant to change

5. High stakes—managing work with tight deadlines, pressure from above, high visibility, and responsibility for critical decisions

6. Scope and scale—managing work that is broad in scope (involving multiple functions, groups, locations, products, or services) or large in size (related to workload, number of responsibilities, and those sorts of things)

7. External pressure—managing the interface with important groups outside the organization, such as customers, vendors, partners, unions, and regulatory agencies

8. Influence without authority—influencing peers, higher management, or other key people over whom you have no authority

9. Work across cultures—working with people from different cultures or with institutions in other countries

10. Work group diversity—being responsible for the work of people of both genders and different racial and ethnic backgrounds.

   (McCauley, 2006)

Using blank copies of the Developmental Job Assignment Worksheet (Exhibit 6.3), you can begin to tailor assignments for specific leaders in your organization. Those assignments can help them build the competencies they need to meet your organization's strategic goals and to close the gap between what is needed and the pool of available leadership talent.

DEVELOPMENTAL RELATIONSHIPS

Relationships, both on and off the job, are central to development. Everyone has known a boss, a mentor, a coach, a peer, an advisor, a role model who influenced his or her thinking about leadership or about what an effective leader does and how an effective leader behaves (some role models are examples of what *not* to do as leaders).

In the Corporate Leadership Council's 2001 Leadership Survey, leader development activities that were grounded in feedback and relationships (mentoring, executive coaching, and interaction with peers, for example) were rated as more effective for development than job experiences and education. Consequently, encouraging either informal or formal relationships is a good strategy for you to consider in developing your organization's leadership talent.

Exhibit 6.2
Sample Developmental Job Assignment Worksheet

Name: Michael   Assignment: Job Rotation in HR

Check each box that applies to this person's assignment.

Developmental Challenges	Not at All Descriptive	Slightly Descriptive	Moderately Descriptive	Very Descriptive	Extremely Descriptive
Unfamiliar Responsibilities					X
New Directions					X
Inherited Problems			X		
Problems with Employees					
High Stakes		X			
Increased Scope and Scale	X				
External Pressure			X		
Influence without Authority			X		
Work Across Cultures			X		
Work Group Diversity			X		

Conclusions/Recommendations:

Exhibit 6.3

Developmental Job Assignment Worksheet

Name:

Assignment:

Check each box that applies to this person's assignment.

Developmental Challenges	Not at All Descriptive	Slightly Descriptive	Moderately Descriptive	Very Descriptive	Extremely Descriptive
Unfamiliar Responsibilities					
New Directions					
Inherited Problems					
Problems with Employees					
High Stakes					
Increased Scope and Scale					
External Pressure					
Influence without Authority					
Work Across Cultures					
Work Group Diversity					

Conclusions/Recommendations:

Of all potentially developmental relationships, the boss-direct report relationship is the most important, for better or worse (Corporate Leadership Council, 2001). Fully 90 percent of the other people who influence an individual in his or her career are bosses (McCall, Lombardo, & Morrison, 1988). That makes it critical for you to involve managers in your DLT strategy, so that they can help their direct reports prepare effective development plans and therefore to develop.

Informal relationships, those that occur as part of the regular workday and are not structured or planned, are natural ways to learn and grow. Such things as informal networks, spontaneous chats in the hallway or over lunch, or peer feedback can be beneficial (McCauley & Douglas, 2004).

Formal relationships are those that are initiated by the organization for the express purpose of development (e.g., mentoring, assignment of an executive coach). A manager should also encourage a subordinate to seek out individuals both internal and external to the organization as a way of gathering feedback and perspective (colleagues, friends in other industries, spouses, a mentor in a volunteer organization, etc.). Informally, individuals who are self-motivated to development may seek out individuals from whom they can learn and gain insight as well as tap into their networks.

Exhibit 6.4 is a worksheet to help you think through how you might connect people in developmental relationships and what roles they could play in the leader's development. Whatever balance you decide on between formal and informal developmental relationships, it is important that you involve the organization in supplying the resources for encouraging both. The organization can help by creating an environment that encourages people to seek out developmental relationships and rewarding them for it. For example, the organization or individual managers can:

- Endorse the idea that seeking out developmental relationships is important and expected.

- Empower individuals to seek out developmental tactics that are most useful for them.

- Ensure that spontaneous and informal developmental relationships are acknowledged and recorded in annual performance appraisals as a contribution to development.

Also consider that, traditionally, formal developmental relationships were made available mainly to white males. While this issue may now have been addressed

Exhibit 6.4

Developmental Relationships Worksheet

Name: _____

Development Goal: _____

	NAMES / ROLES							
Assessment	Feedback Provider							
	Sounding Board							
	Point of Comparison							
	Feedback Interpreter							
Challenge	Dialogue Partner							
	Assignment Broker							
	Accountant							
	Role Model							
Support	Counselor							
	Cheerleader							
	Reinforcer							
	Cohort							

from a "policy" perspective in many organizations, when it comes to the "practices" of development, established systems may still not provide the type of cultural background understanding useful to both the mentor and mentee (see Exhibit 6.5). That's why informal relationships, predominately driven by networking, become critically important.

STRUCTURED DEVELOPMENT PROGRAMS

In addressing their need for leadership talent, many organizations make use of universities, consultants, and other training and education providers. These kinds of initiatives usually focus on knowledge acquisition and perhaps some

Exhibit 6.5
Barriers to Effective Mentoring

Traditionally, mentoring opportunities were limited mainly to white male managers. Even in today's diverse workplaces, formal mentoring programs may not be able to overcome cultural background differences in developmental relationships (see, for example, Livers & Caver, 2003, 2004). Many non-white and female managers will have issues that are outside the scope of concerns of many white male mentors. For example, female managers often feel that they are held to higher standards. The same work for the same job does not get them to the same place as their male counterparts go. Ethnic and racial minorities often report similar obstacles, and these issues are compounded when there also are generational differences between the mentor and manager in a developmental relationship.

Other concerns for these managers include feeling more closely scrutinized for mistakes, the sense that information to which others may have free access is withheld, a fear of being labeled incompetent, receiving less feedback, and weaker internal networks.

All of these factors complicate the developmental aspects of mentoring relationships. Be sure to take age, culture, gender, language, and other differences into consideration when developing the part of your plan that calls for developmental relationships.

degree of guided skill application (see Chapter 5 for a more detailed explanation of developmental levels).

To make structured development programs most effective, however, other elements are required: the developmental infrastructure of assessment, challenge, and support and a feedback-intensive component. A feedback-intensive program is one that contains a comprehensive assessment of an individual's leadership, generally in one or more sessions, using multiple lenses to view numerous aspects of personality and effectiveness (Guthrie & King, 2004).

Multi-rater (360-degree) feedback instruments are quite effective in providing those multiple lenses. This method systematically collects opinions about an individual's performance from a wide range of co-workers, including peers, subordinates, bosses, and people outside of the organization. Usually, a facilitator helps the person being developed understand the results and develop a plan for moving forward.

Table 6.1 lists some of the activities typically found in feedback-intensive programs. As in other elements of the DLT approach, assessment, challenge, and support provide a framework for the activities and should be integrated in preprogram and postprogram activities, as well as throughout the program.

Best Practices for Selecting or Developing Structured Development Programs

There are several best practices to follow in selecting or developing structured development programs, shown on the following list. Structured programs are most effective when they are built around a well-delineated leadership model and combined with other development strategies, such as coaching and learning on the job. Clear-cut participant selection criteria, required prework, and personalized feedback to reinforce learning are also key considerations as is a design that incorporates multiple learning sessions over an extended time. Additionally, participants in a structured program should be there because they want to attend. It is difficult to get the commitment needed for learning and development without the desire.

Best Practices for Selecting or Designing Effective Development Programs

- Build around a single well-delineated leadership model.
- Use a participant selection process with clear criteria.
- Conduct pre-course preparation.
- Use personalized 360-degree feedback to reinforce learning.
- Use multiple learning methods.
- Conduct extended learning periods and multiple sessions over time.

Additional Considerations When Designing Your Own Structured Program

To address the specific needs of your organization, you may decide to develop your own training program. Note that common shortcomings of structured programs include:

- Failure to build sustainable levels of interest and support
- Shortcomings of competency-based leadership models

Table 6.1
Feedback-Intensive Program Activities

Phase	Assessment Activities	Challenge Activities	Support Activities
Preprogram	• Personality measures • 360-degree feedback • Leadership instruments • Open-ended, essay-type questions • Qualitative reports by participants about challenges • Interviews with boss • Preparation of business cases or projects	• Completing personality and leadership measures • Writing essays, doing interviews, and preparing cases challenge individuals to think about their views on self, organization, and leadership	• Staff contacts with each participant to provide information, answer questions, and clarify expectations
Program	Methodologies for assessment: • Reflection • Participant observations • Staff observations • Videotape	A variety of teaching tools and delivery methods: • Assessments • Lecturettes • Discussions • Simulations • Exercises • Different viewpoints and mental models • Nontraditional techniques (acting, music, collage, and so on)	Staff-created learning community: • Cooperative developmental environment • Appropriate self-disclosure • Respect and openness • Authenticity • Nonprescriptive and nonjudgmental commentary • No right answers • Respectful work with each person • Positive climate
Postprogram	• Repeat of multi-rater or 360-degree feedback • Instruments to assess behavior change • Feedback coaches	• Learning partners • Feedback coaches	• In-class learning partners • Feedback coaches • Back-home learning groups • Alumni groups • Blended learning • Succession and development-planning processes

Source: Guthrie, V. A., & King, S. N. (2004). "Feedback-Intensive Programs." In C. D. McCauley & E. Van Velsor, *The Center for Creative Leadership Handbook of Leadership Development* (2nd ed., p. 29). San Francisco: Jossey-Bass.

- Insufficient time spent on developing individual skill areas

- Limited or no program follow-up

- Few or no links to job assignments

To be successful in custom designing a structured program for your organization, in addition to following the best practices outlined earlier, you must fully understand the needs of the target population. The conceptual framework of your program, its content, and the placement of exercises and assessments must match and reflect the complexity and turbulence participants experience, be relevant to their leadership challenges, and be action-oriented (Guthrie & King, 2004). For example, a program for entry-level managers might be aimed at helping them learn to influence others and build credibility for their management skills. A program for mid-level managers may be focused on developing others and maintaining life balance.

360-DEGREE FEEDBACK TOOLS

Formal 360-degree feedback provides something that informal feedback seldom does: a structured means of collecting and processing data and an opportunity to reflect on this valuable information. It may be the only time some leaders ever consciously stop to take stock of their performance effectiveness in an organized way.

Research shows that 360-degree feedback can improve performance and lead to behavior change over time (Atwater, Waldman, Atwater, & Cartier, 2000; Smither, London, & Richmond, 2005; Walker & Smither, 1999). In addition to its use in developing individual competency, organizations also use 360-degree feedback to determine group strengths and development needs. Compiling individual feedback results into an aggregate group profile can inform a company what competencies it would like to maintain or develop further. Used in this way, the 360 process would be relevant to the competency modeling and gap analysis aspects of the DLT approach.

The ratings for 360-degree feedback are collected anonymously (that is, the participant cannot tell who provided the ratings), with the exception of supervisor ratings. Because most people have only one boss, it is difficult, if not impossible, to keep supervisor ratings anonymous.

With 360-degree feedback, the assessment of an individual's strengths and development needs is more reliable and valid because of multiple raters. Typical 360 tools have supervisors, peers, direct reports, the participant, and others complete valid and reliable surveys on which they rate (or assess) the behavior and other attributes of the participant using numerical rating scales. Multiple raters provide different perspectives on an individual's performance, making the feedback more accurate and more useful to the recipient. By collecting feedback from several different individuals with different relationships to the recipient, the effect of personal biases is significantly decreased.

Facilitation sessions are critical to help participants identify goals for needed behavior change. Brutus and Derayeh (2002) report that every organization in their study that failed to meet the objectives of the 360 process had failed to facilitate the feedback process. In these organizations, participants received reports in the mail without individual or group facilitation with a trained feedback coach. The organizations that were successful in meeting their objectives for the program were the ones that facilitated the feedback process.

Facilitation sessions are essential when 360 feedback is used as a leadership development strategy. The impact of 360-degree feedback can be even more significant when combined with other methodologies such as a structured learning program or working with a coach. If you want more guidance on the use of 360-degree feedback in the leadership development process, we recommend *Leveraging the Impact of 360-Degree Feedback,* in which our colleagues John Fleenor, Sylvester Taylor, and Craig Chappelow (2008) draw from the lessons learned through research and practice at CCL going back to the mid-1970s.

A final word: Careful attention to the underlying principles of the DLT approach can close the leadership gap in your organization by helping you select the right mix of developmental experiences for your target audience. In creating that mix, you increase your chances of success by adhering to the research-based maxim that people in organizations learn best from their experiences and acknowledging that development is an ongoing process of learning and change. Building a program that includes such strategies as developmental job assignments and similar experiences can help to ensure that it produces the results your organization needs.

Development Strategies Checklist

What learning activities will work best in your organization to close the gap? *What development methods will you use and why?*

- Which method or combination of methods would be most effective in closing the gaps you have identified (methods include such things as cross-functional projects, developmental job assignments, coaching, and formal assessments)?

- Is your organization ready to proceed with a development initiative? How ready are those who must support the development effort? If you do not know, how will you determine readiness?

- What organizational constraints (for example, time, money, facility use, administrative support) must you account for when choosing methodologies?

- What worked well in the past? What contributed to the success? Is it applicable to the current situation?

- What did not work well in the past? What contributed to its failure? How will you ensure that the current program is not tainted by association?

Implementation

E ven the best of plans cannot anticipate every problem. The real test comes when it is time to implement the design. That is the subject of this chapter.

Your essential task at this stage of the DLT process is to plan the implementation of the design of your development process and discern any resistance that the organization might have to it. Additionally, you should continue to seek and bolster support from senior leaders in the organization.

THINKING ABOUT IMPLEMENTATION

We've been using the ACS model (see Chapter 1) to organize your thinking in relation to several important aspects of a leadership development process (see Figure 7.1). The elements of ACS increase the chances that a developmental experience will have an impact on leaders. ACS motivates people to focus their attention and efforts on learning, growth, and change. It can also be used to think about issues related to implementation.

When we ask participants and clients what gets in the way of implementation, they frequently cite reasons like the following organizational issues:

- Support for the development initiative wanes after the "kick-off" phase.
- The development initiative is not integrated with other talent management functions.
- The organization does not honor leadership development as a competitive advantage and so the initiative lacks credibility.

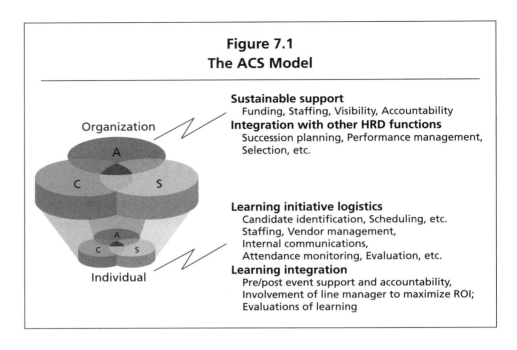

Figure 7.1
The ACS Model

Organization

A

C S

Sustainable support
Funding, Staffing, Visibility, Accountability
Integration with other HRD functions
Succession planning, Performance management,
Selection, etc.

Learning initiative logistics
Candidate identification, Scheduling, etc.
Staffing, Vendor management,
Internal communications,
Attendance monitoring, Evaluation, etc.
Learning integration
Pre/post event support and accountability,
Involvement of line manager to maximize ROI;
Evaluations of learning

A

C S

Individual

Program participants and clients also cite the following individual-level examples of difficulties they encounter when implementing the development strategy:

- Not involving and preparing the managers of the individuals undergoing development for their ongoing support and accountability.

- Naive expectations that exposure to learning means the participant has integrated and can apply the learning.

- The individual learner is either overwhelmed with other work demands or loses interest in the development process.

Thinking in terms of the ACS model and using (or adapting) the DLT methods and tools we suggest makes it possible to anticipate and even avert many of these implementation pitfalls. One way to check whether you and your organization have covered most of the bases is to pause long enough in the DLT planning process to perform a Developmental Climate Audit (see Exhibit 7.1). Your assessment at that point will let you know whether conditions in your organization are favorable enough to proceed or whether you have to build additional support for your development initiative.

Exhibit 7.1
Developmental Climate Audit

For each statement indicate whether it reflects conditions in your organization, using the following response options:

1=Strongly disagree	2=Disagree	3=Neither agree nor disagree	4=Agree	5=Strongly agree

Leadership Competencies

1.	We have identified a core list of leadership competencies.	1	2	3	4	5
2.	Among the core list of competencies we have identified *specific* leadership competencies that are necessary to meet strategic and competitive challenges.	1	2	3	4	5
3.	We have assessed the relative importance and strength of these competencies in our organization as a whole.	1	2	3	4	5
4.	We have assessed the relative importance and strength of these competencies in individuals.	1	2	3	4	5

Assessment

5.	We provide frequent and honest feedback to people about their strengths and weaknesses.	1	2	3	4	5
6.	We have formal performance management processes that provide people with accurate data on their work performance.	1	2	3	4	5
7.	People work with their bosses to identify development needs and plans to address those needs.	1	2	3	4	5

Challenge

8.	We frequently provide people opportunities to stretch and develop early in their careers.	1	2	3	4	5
9.	We sometimes put people in jobs for development even if they are not necessarily "best" qualified.	1	2	3	4	5
10.	We encourage people to seek out and learn from new experiences and new people.	1	2	3	4	5
11.	We encourage people to set difficult goals or tackle tough problems.	1	2	3	4	5
12.	To get the job done, people often have to work with others who bring quite different perspectives to the table (e.g., perspectives from different functions, business units, or geographical areas).	1	2	3	4	5

(Continued)

1=Strongly disagree	2=Disagree	3=Neither agree nor disagree	4=Agree	5=Strongly agree

Support

		1	2	3	4	5
13.	People are quick to take on coaching and mentoring roles for others in the organization.	1	2	3	4	5
14.	The importance of developing people at all levels is a basic belief in our organization.	1	2	3	4	5
15.	People have the freedom to pursue learning and development goals.	1	2	3	4	5
16.	We help people learn from their mistakes.	1	2	3	4	5
17.	We believe that a person's development is a joint responsibility of the individual and the organization.	1	2	3	4	5
18.	Our managers receive specific training on how to be effective at developmental coaching.	1	2	3	4	5

Priority of Senior Management

		1	2	3	4	5
19.	Our CEO has a real commitment to the development of people and makes that commitment apparent.	1	2	3	4	5
20.	The development of employees is a key part of our overall business strategy.	1	2	3	4	5
21.	Line managers consider "developing others" to be a part of their regular job.	1	2	3	4	5
22.	We do not let short-term business pressure interfere with our development of people.	1	2	3	4	5

Recognition and Rewards

		1	2	3	4	5
23.	Good performance and high potential are recognized and rewarded.	1	2	3	4	5
24.	We reward people who develop the talents and skills needed for effectiveness in the organization.	1	2	3	4	5
25.	We use pay to differentiate among people — we give larger rewards for better performance and vice versa.	1	2	3	4	5
26.	Politics do not play much of a role in decisions about people.	1	2	3	4	5

Regular Communication

		1	2	3	4	5
27.	Employee talents and performance are highlighted in the organization's formal communication channel.	1	2	3	4	5
28.	People can readily access information about development strategies and opportunities in the organization.	1	2	3	4	5

1=Strongly disagree	2=Disagree	3=Neither agree nor disagree	4=Agree	5=Strongly agree

Efforts to Track and Measure

29.	We have identified specific competencies we need to develop in our organization.	1	2	3	4	5
30.	We have organizational metrics for tracking whether we are developing the leadership talent we need.	1	2	3	4	5
31.	Formal development initiatives are regularly evaluated as part of efforts to enhance their effectiveness.	1	2	3	4	5
32.	Bosses monitor employees' progress on developmental goals.	1	2	3	4	5

Processes and Resources to Support

33.	We have identified key transition points for career development in our organization.	1	2	3	4	5
34.	We plan development activities for the key points in a career where they can have the most impact.	1	2	3	4	5
35.	We use many different development methods and tools.	1	2	3	4	5
36.	We are willing to move aside "adequate" performers to unclog the channels for more talented up-and-comers.	1	2	3	4	5
37.	We take a long-term perspective when planning for development — five or ten years out, not just tomorrow.	1	2	3	4	5
38.	Our human resource policies and practices are designed to meet both the individual's and the organization's needs.	1	2	3	4	5
39.	Our human resource processes (compensation, benefits, etc.) all work together to support people development.	1	2	3	4	5

Employee Knowledge and Skills

40.	We put considerable emphasis on recruiting and selecting the right people to work in our organization.	1	2	3	4	5
41.	We attract people who are learning oriented and motivated to expand their capabilities.	1	2	3	4	5
42.	The ability to learn, grow, and adapt to new situations is valued among employees.	1	2	3	4	5

Another useful exercise for many leadership development professionals is to summarize all their data-gathering, assessment, and design work into a DLT proposal document (see Exhibit 7.2).

**Exhibit 7.2
DLT Planning Worksheet (Proposal Outline)**

PRELIMINARY INPUT
Enter your notes for input on each of the planning categories in the pages below.

WHY—PURPOSE

WHAT—CONTENT

ORGANIZATION CAPABILITY

How/logistics—The nuts and bolts of how you will implement your plan

How/content—The content and methodology to deliver the content of your development initiative

Relationships—Interpersonal relations with key stakeholders and others (can also use stakeholder analysis)

EVALUATION—ASSESSMENT
MAKE THE CASE

Why is development needed—from a business/organization perspective?

What capabilities and competencies have to be developed?

How will this development build both individual and organizational capability?

To what level(s) of proficiency?

In what parts of the organization?

Who will be developed—individuals/employee groups and functions (connect to *what* and *why*)?

(*Continued*)

IMPLEMENTATION PLANNING TEMPLATE

Who	Project Task	mm/yy	mm/yy	mm/yy	mm/yy	mm/yy
	1.					
	1.1					
	1.2					
	1.3					
	1.4					
	2.					
	2.1					
	2.2					
	2.3					
	2.4					
	Etc.					

PLAN OVERVIEW

You have completed Why, What, and Who will be developed.

You have completed the detailed implementation plan—you know the potential barriers and constraints.

What is/are the development methodologies?

How do they link with and support Why, What, Who?

How do they fit within organizational constraints?

Now, prepare a broad plan that summarizes the case and links it to development methodologies. This can be your complete proposal document.

GARNERING SUPPORT AND MANAGING RESISTANCE

In leading up to implementation, you will have addressed strategy, skills needed, gaps, and target populations. All of these elements are critical for creating and then implementing your organization's leadership development strategy. And as you do these things you also should be developing and maintaining the support of key stakeholders.

Do not mistake your organization's initial interest or even its demands for developing leadership as an indication that it will support what you design. When it comes to devoting time, taking people off their regular work assignments, and budgeting money to the process, it is not uncommon to experience some resistance. You must take into consideration the political realities of your organization. It is important to ensure that you have identified your critical stakeholders and are prepared to manage any resistance that may be encountered.

In his book *The Empowered Manager*, Peter Block (1991) provides a simple and useful framework for thinking about your stakeholders that we have adapted for use in our own practices.

In this framework there are two important variables to take into consideration when thinking about your stakeholders: agreement and trust. What is the level of agreement between you and your stakeholders when it comes to the design you have created (need for it, target population, and so on)? What is the level of trust between you and your stakeholders?

When combined, these variables help to identify five categories of stakeholders: Allies, Opponents, Associates, Adversaries, and Undecided (Figure 7.2). By applying this framework to your circumstances, you can begin to identify and think about those individuals who may either support or resist the development strategy you have designed.

You can use the Stakeholder Analysis Worksheet (Exhibit 7.3) to think through the levels of support and resistance facing your development initiative and record your conclusions. If you use the worksheet to focus on specific areas of support and specific pockets of resistance, you will be better able to marshal and target your responses and influence to overcome the barriers.

With careful analysis and forethought, resistance from your opponents—and sometimes even adversaries—can be countered and often overcome. Some objections, such as "leading a global team is no different from leading a regular team," can be answered with education. Other reasons for opposing your initiative, such as a shortage of resources, may require lining up support from your

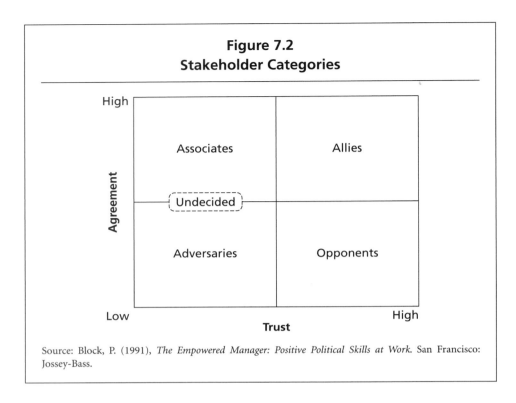

Figure 7.2
Stakeholder Categories

Associates	Allies
Undecided	
Adversaries	Opponents

Agreement (High / Low) — Trust (Low / High)

Source: Block, P. (1991), *The Empowered Manager: Positive Political Skills at Work.* San Francisco: Jossey-Bass.

strongest allies or the skillful use of influence and political savvy. One especially useful tactic is to reframe an objection so that it becomes supportive. For example, a unit that devotes resources to securing the technology needed to support global teams can become an important developmental channel for leaders who want to build that competency.

A final word: In a perfect world, your organization has a clear strategy; it knows it needs leadership to reach its strategic goals; it realizes that it has skill and competency gaps in the leadership it currently has; and it accepts the idea that developing leaders is a way of reaching a desired state of sustainability.

The reality is that not everyone will embrace your ideas for leadership development. Some executives in your organization may agree that development is needed but disagree with your plan. Others in the organization may directly or indirectly disagree with both the need for development and your recommendations.

Having a clear picture of the developmental climate in your organization and making a persuasive case for the proposed leadership development, from a business/organization perspective, can help you navigate the resistance that

Exhibit 7.3
Stakeholder Analysis Worksheet

Identify people within your organization who are or could be stakeholders in your development initiative. Place them in one of the stakeholder categories and determine the most effective way to deal with them to win support, minimize opposition, etc.

Allies—Individuals who fully agree with your thinking, strategy, and implementation plans.

Opponents—Individuals who generally agree with your position, but not with your strategy or implementation plans.

Associates—Individuals who generally agree with your thinking, strategy, and implementation plans.

Adversaries—Individuals who disagree with your thinking, strategy, and implementation plans. There are also issues of trust.

Undecided—Individuals who may be open to your influence; you must sell them on your thinking, strategy, and implementation plans.

might sink the effort before it starts. One final recommendation: Don't ignore the "undecideds." Devoting time and energy to converting them to associates or even allies could add significant weight to the organizational support for your leadership development plans and ensure your eventual success.

Implementation Checklist

What are the logistics involved with implementing your organization's leader-development process? *How will you implement your development initiative?*

- Who has a stake in this leader-development initiative? To what degree will they support or challenge it?

- What resources will be needed to implement this leader-development initiative (for example, time, money, project management)?

- How will your initiative be integrated with other elements of your organization's talent-management system (including previous leader-development activities)?

- How will managers be held accountable for the development of their direct reports?

- When will your leader-development initiative start and when will it end?

Ongoing Evaluation

Anecdotal information about your leadership development program, even when it comes as sincere and insightful feedback, cannot replace the need for a high-quality evaluation. Given the approach you have taken to identify organizational needs and leadership capacity, you will want to know (and senior leadership in your organizations will want to know) whether or not the program you are running is closing the gaps. Your organization will be specifically interested to see if its investment is paying off.

It is often difficult to identify the most critical factors to evaluate in a leader-development process. Isolating the effects of leader development from other forces also acting on the organization is quite complex. This chapter describes a model for evaluation driven by three principles:

- Evaluation work should be participatory,
- It should be integrated with initiative design, and
- It should enhance organizational learning.

A *participatory approach* means that all relevant stakeholders are involved in the planning or are informed about it. *Integration with initiative design* means that the focus and design of an evaluation are incorporated into the design of the initiative process being evaluated. *Organizational learning* is reflected in the organization's increased knowledge about whether an initiative has been successful or not and what needs to change as a result or what needs to be enhanced (Hannum & Martineau, 2008; Martineau, 2004).

In our own DLT work and the discussion here, we rely heavily on the evaluation material written by our CCL colleagues Jennifer Martineau and Kelly Hannum because their work is specifically focused on evaluating leadership development programs. In *Evaluating the Impact of Leadership Development* (2008), they explain in depth how to use the evaluation processes and tools we recommend.

Keep in mind that even though evaluation is the last piece of our DLT approach, activities involved in evaluation are not left until last. In practice, you should give careful thought to evaluation issues from the moment you begin thinking about your organization's process for developing leadership talent.

A FRAMEWORK FOR EVALUATION

In 1975, Donald Kirkpatrick first presented a four-level model of evaluation that has become a classic in the industry:

- *Level One: Reaction*—Evaluating the training after completing the program—for example, rating forms sometimes called *smile sheets.*
- *Level Two: Learning*—Evaluating how much was actually learned—for example, with pre- and posttests.
- *Level Three: Behavior*—Evaluating whether behavior actually changes as a result of learning—for example, by testing three to six months after the event.
- *Level Four: Results*—Evaluating the business impact—determining, for example, whether the training actually produced sales results or fewer defects in products.

In our view, evaluation helps people in organizations meet several goals. It helps them make informed decisions about how to improve development initiatives and helps them examine the degree to which development goals have been achieved. An underlying assumption in the DLT approach is that change is constant and that any evaluation system should be fluid enough to accommodate the frequent transitions that accompany organizational life.

There are three major phases to the DLT framework for evaluation:

1. Focusing the evaluation
2. Designing and conducting the evaluation
3. Using evaluation findings

FOCUSING THE EVALUATION

The ideal time to plan an evaluation is when the development initiative is being designed. That way, you can focus the evaluation on stakeholder expectations. It is also important to take into consideration the patterns and the pace of work in the organization. For instance, there may be times (during budget planning, for example) that are not optimal for evaluation activities.

There are several actions you can take to focus your evaluation. The questions listed are intended as guidance; adapt them or add others to fit your situation.

Identify Stakeholders

Who has an interest in the development initiative? Who has an interest in the evaluation's processes and results? Are there additional people whose support is required for the success of the initiative or the evaluation? Who has decision-making authority with respect to both the initiative and the evaluation? Who will be affected by the development initiative and its evaluation?

By following the DLT approach, you have already answered some of these questions. You can use the Stakeholder Evaluation Issues Worksheet in Exhibit 8.1 to focus your thoughts on stakeholder concerns with respect to the evaluation of your leadership development initiative.

Define Purpose

What is the reason behind the development initiative? For example, are stakeholders generally content with the organization's leadership but seeking a standard of leadership practice? Do stakeholders want a program of development in order to create and reinforce a new and different set of skills? What specific business challenges does the organization hope to address by setting up this initiative? How does this initiative support the organization's business strategy? What specific leadership needs does this initiative address? Are there any other external and internal pressures or demands for creating this initiative?

The Evaluation Purpose Definition Worksheet (Exhibit 8.2) is a place to organize your thinking on these and other questions from an evaluation perspective.

Establish the Desired Types of Impact and Time Frame

Is the development initiative expected to have an impact on individuals, groups, or the organization? Is the development initiative expected to have short-term, midrange, or long-term impact?

Exhibit 8.1
Stakeholder Evaluation Issues Worksheet

List and describe the stakeholders who are involved in the development initiative or have an interest in the outcome of the initiative or its evaluation. In identifying stakeholder position or description, include such people as the designers of the initiative, trainers, human resources staff, potential participants, community leaders, senior managers or political leaders concerned with the results, managers whose staff will participate in the initiative, and the group or groups funding the initiative.

Who has an interest in the development initiative?
Name:
Stakeholder position/description:
Stakeholder interest:

Who has an interest in the evaluation's processes and results?
Name:
Stakeholder position/description:
Stakeholder interest:

Are there additional people whose support (financial, political, organizational, etc.) is required for the success of the initiative or the evaluation?
Name:
Stakeholder position/description:
Stakeholder interest:

Who has decision-making authority with respect to both the initiative and the evaluation?
Name:
Stakeholder position/description:
Stakeholder interest:

_____

Adapted from K. Hannum and J. W. Martineau (2008), *Evaluating the Impact of Leadership Development.* San Francisco: Pfeiffer.

Exhibit 8.2
Evaluation Purpose Definition Worksheet

Seek answers to these questions from the initiative's key stakehold-ers before designing your evaluation plan. The answers will help you define what stakeholders see as the purpose of the development initia-tive. With that information you can focus your evaluation to measure expected results.

What specific challenge is the initiative expected to address?

How does this initiative support the organization's business strategy or the community or social change strategy?

What specific leadership needs does this initiative address?

What are the purposes of the leadership development intervention(s)? For example, are stakeholders generally content with the status quo of the organization's leadership but seeking a standard of leadership prac-tice? Do stakeholders want a program of development in order to cre-ate and reinforce a new and different set of skills?

Are there any other external and internal pressures or demands for cre-ating this initiative?

Will participants be held accountable for their development as a result of this initiative? If so, how?

What level of accomplishment is the initiative intended to promote? Knowledge acquisition? Awareness change? Behavioral change? Skill development? Performance improvement?

What type of impact is the initiative expected to have? Will it affect only individuals? Will it affect teams or groups? Will it have broad organizational or community impact?

How will the information in the initiative be delivered and over what span of time? Will it be a single five-day session or two three-day sessions held six months apart? Will it include online components?

What data will be collected during the initiative that may be useful in an evaluation? What data are being collected by others that may be useful in an evaluation?

What evaluation techniques, such as end-of-program surveys, are already designed for or in use by the initiative?

Adapted from K. Hannum and J. W. Martineau (2008), *Evaluating the Impact of Leadership Development.* San Francisco: Pfeiffer.

Uncover Expectations

What is anticipated to occur as a result of your development initiative and its evaluation? What specific behaviors do stakeholders expect participants to exhibit as a result? What specific outcomes do stakeholders expect? Over what span of time is the program to occur? What evidence of impact will the stakeholders consider necessary to believe that the intended outcomes have been achieved? What type of data will they accept, and what sources will they trust?

Use the Evaluation Expectations Worksheet (Exhibit 8.3) to organize your answers and conclusions.

Determine Resources

How much time, money, and staff will be needed for the evaluation? When are stakeholders expecting to see results? Who is available to perform the evaluation? How much data will be collected during the evaluation? How will the organization put the evaluation results to use?

The cost of evaluating your DLT initiative depends on the complexity of the initiative and the evaluation. For example, if stakeholders want to measure results at multiple stages, you will require more resources than for a single effort to collect the necessary data, analyze it, and communicate the results. As a general rule, evaluations typically take up 5 percent to 20 percent of the cost of a development initiative (Hannum & Martineau, 2008).

Determine Evaluation Questions

How will you reflect stakeholder expectations in your evaluation questions? When are answers to those questions expected? What types of impact and what time frame are of interest to stakeholders? How will the information from the evaluation be used?

Sample questions to consider covering in your evaluation design include:

- To what extent does the leadership development initiative meet its stated objectives?

- Are there any unintended benefits or challenges raised by the initiative?

- To what degree are participants prepared to apply what they have learned to their work?

Exhibit 8.3
Evaluation Expectations Worksheet

Use this worksheet to specify implicit and explicit expectations so that you can take them into account during the design phase. If you work with different stakeholder groups separately, you may have to change the focus based on what is relevant for each person or group. If it is possible, it can be helpful for the different stakeholder groups to get together at the same time to discuss expectations.

What specific outcomes have stakeholders said they expect in order to consider the initiative a success?

Identify specific behaviors that stakeholders expect participants to exhibit as a result of this initiative.

How are these behaviors different from or similar to current behaviors being exhibited?

Is there baseline information about participants' current behavior? (Review previous assessment activities, if available.)

What are the implications of not pursuing a development initiative or an evaluation?

(Continued)

Over what period of time is the initiative to occur?

When do stakeholders expect the initiative to have its desired impact? (How much time will they allow before they expect to see the desired change?)

What questions will stakeholders and others ask about the effectiveness of the evaluation?

What evidence of impact will the stakeholders consider necessary to believe that the intended outcomes have been achieved? What type of data will they accept (qualitative or quantitative)? What sources will they trust (for example, participants, their managers, their clients)?

How do stakeholders expect results to be communicated (final evaluation report, update memos, etc.)?

Adapted from K. Hannum and J. W. Martineau (2008), *Evaluating the Impact of Leadership Development.* San Francisco: Pfeiffer.

- To what degree have participants applied what they have learned to their work?

- To what extent have participants made significant behavioral changes?

- What is the impact of participants' behavioral changes (or other changes) on those around them?

- Has the organization or community experienced the intended changes (benefits) as a result of the initiative?

Use the worksheet in Exhibit 8.4 to focus your thinking about what questions to cover in your evaluation.

Determine Sample and Methods

Identifying your sample and choosing a data-collection method are the last two tasks in focusing your evaluation. You might want to start by reviewing your list of stakeholders, and then determine whether you want to collect data from the entire group or from a sample. For example, information about the trainers' behavior in the classroom may best be collected from participants because other stakeholders are unlikely to have information. Conversely, participants may not have information about such matters as the relationship of organizational HR policies to leadership development success.

Some critical questions at this stage are: What information is needed? What are the underlying questions that have to be answered? And what kind of information is needed? That is, do you want to know whether training objectives were achieved, whether learning was accomplished, whether there was a return on investment?

As to the data-collection method, no single method (survey, interview, observation, or assessment instrument) can fully garner a complete picture from the respondents. The unit of measurement for the evaluation can be the individual, group or team, and organization or community. Here are some sample evaluation methods for each:

Individual-Level Impact

- End-of-program evaluations

- Interviews

- Retrospective 360-degree feedback

Exhibit 8.4
Evaluation Questions Worksheet

Use this worksheet to determine and define questions to use in your evaluation.

What are the critical questions the evaluation should answer?

From whose perspective are the questions being posed?

When are answers to those questions expected?

What are the objectives of the development initiative?

What aspects of the initiative address those objectives?

What logical connections can be made (or should be investigated) between initiative outcomes and the intended impact?

What types of impact and what time frame are of interest to stakeholders?

What outcomes are possible to measure, given the timing of the evaluation in relation to the implementation of the initiative?

What elements of context are important to understand?

How will information from the evaluation be used?

Adapted from K. Hannum and J. W. Martineau (2008), *Evaluating the Impact of Leadership Development*. San Francisco: Pfeiffer.

Team-Level Impact

- Focus group
- Project documentation
- Behavioral observations

Organizational-Level Impact

- Climate surveys and retest
- Project documentation
- Observations
- Organizational measures
- Customer satisfaction

It is best to use more than one method. This allows the strengths of one method to compensate for the weakness of another. Also, keep in mind that data are either qualitative or quantitative and that it depends on the needs of the audience as to which are more appropriate or what balance between the two can work best.

GUIDELINES FOR DESIGNING AND CONDUCTING THE EVALUATION

The DLT evaluation-design guidelines suggested here will help you improve the quality of the data you collect and present:

- Examine impact from multiple perspectives.
- Assess the different kinds of change that can be observed.
- Use multiple data-collection methods.
- Look at change over time.
- Assess individual and group-level change.
- Use control groups for comparison.
- Use time-series designs for comparison.

When you design your evaluation plan, it is not necessary at this stage to have identified specific content. Your intent should be to choose methods that are likely to produce the type of data valued by key stakeholders. Your plan should provide an overview of data-collection activities and demonstrate that you are collecting the appropriate data needed to answer the evaluation questions. For a sample plan template, see Exhibit 8.5.

USING EVALUATION FINDINGS

To ensure that your evaluation findings will be used to support individual, team, and organizational learning, be sure to complete four critical activities: effectively communicate the results, identify specific courses of action, develop a detailed action plan, and monitor the action plan's implementation (see Exhibit 8.6).

These activities create a greater likelihood that your recommendations will be carefully considered and translated into realistic actions for the individuals and the organization.

A note about producing the final evaluation report: It should be clearly written, to the point, and understandable to a layperson. Headings you can use to organize this report are

- Executive Summary
- Purpose of the Evaluation
- Description of Initiative and Sample
- Caveats About the Evaluation
- Overview of Processes Used and Analysis
- Summary of Data
- Conclusions and Recommendations
- Appendices

A final word: Evaluation can and should be used at any time to calibrate the level of success of a leadership development process. You can use the evaluation techniques outlined in this chapter before designing leadership development tools, for instance, or you can build evaluation into the development intervention itself so that it becomes a way to measure progress. Either way, following the DLT approach will help you consolidate the information you need to design a robust and useful evaluation of your process for developing leadership talent.

Exhibit 8.5
Evaluation Plan Design Example

	Questions	Data-Collection Timing	Participants	Trainers	Coordinators	Sales Staff
PILOT PHASE ONLY	How effective is the current logistical support? How well are program processes (advance information for participants, test administration process, program set-up, etc.) functioning in the multiple locations?	During and immediately after the program		Program debrief	Program debrief	
	Do program staff and faculty have the information and resources they need to provide the highest-quality program? What's helpful? What's missing?	During and immediately after the program		Program debrief	Program debrief	
	Why do participants select this program? What appeals to them about the program? What doesn't appeal to them?		Focus groups			Focus groups
	Is the flow of the program logical and helpful to participants?	Immediately after the program	Focus groups	Program debrief	Program debrief	
	Are all aspects of the program functioning as intended (in order to meet objectives)?	Immediately after the program				
	Pilot Phase Communication Plan: • Written report and presentation to program design team (including trainers) two weeks after the program • Tailored summary of lessons learned to sales staff one or two days after presentation to program design team • Tailored summaries of lessons learned to participants and coordinators one month after the program					

STANDARD EVALUTION PROCESS	To what extent does the program meet the stated objectives?	Immediately after the program	End-of-program survey		
	To what extent are the program objectives relevant?	Immediately after the program	End-of-program survey		
	What are the changes in the selected competencies?	Three months after the program	360-degree retrospective pre/post survey		
	What is the impact on the participants' organizations?	Three months and six months after the program	360-degree retrospective pre/post survey and impact survey		
	Are there any unintended consequences of the program?	Six months after the program	Impact survey		
	What are the barriers and supports for making changes?	Six months after the program	Impact survey		
	Ongoing Communication Plan: • End-of-program survey to trainers and coordinators immediately • Quarterly summary reports of end-of-program survey data to program manager • Individual 360-degree reports to participants the day after data-collection deadline • Semiannual aggregate 360-degree report to program manager				

Adapted from K. Hannum and J. W. Martineau (2008), *Evaluating the Impact of Leadership Development*. San Francisco: Pfeiffer.

Exhibit 8.6
Using Evaluation Findings Checklist

❏ Draft final evaluation report.

❏ Get key stakeholders' feedback on and input to the final report.

❏ Disseminate report through different media.

❏ Determine what changes are needed in what areas.

❏ Examine possible revisions to the initiative and to specific areas that strengthen support structures.

❏ Explore the need to follow up the leadership development initiative with another activity.

❏ Gather and consult with the stakeholders.

❏ Suggest and possibly help develop a detailed action plan.

❏ Suggest and possibly help create a process for monitoring the action plan's implementation.

❏ Suggest ways the evaluation can help create change and learning.

Adapted from K. Hannum and J. W. Martineau (2008), *Evaluating the Impact of Leadership Development*. San Francisco: Pfeiffer.

Ongoing Evaluation Checklist

How will you know whether your leadership development initiative accomplished what you intended it to? *How will you evaluate the impact of your leader-development initiative?*

- What kind of information (for example, qualitative or quantitative data) do you need to accurately evaluate the impact of your development process?

- Do you have processes in place for determining the impact of the development initiative on individuals? On groups and on the organization?

- Can you evaluate the effectiveness of the various components of your development initiative (for example, content, learning methodology, classroom training, online training)?

- How will you know when the gaps you identified have been closed?

- How will you collect enough information to guide you and important stakeholders in designing other development initiatives?

CCL Leadership Competencies List

This list of competencies includes three leadership dimensions: Leading Others, Leading the Organization, and Leading Yourself. The Leading Others dimension contains five factors that reflect one's ability to lead others. The Leading the Organization dimension contains eight factors reflecting one's ability to lead an organization. The Leading Yourself dimension contains seven factors reflecting one's character and ability to manage self and promote self-development.

Leading Others

Factor	Description	Contains These Competencies
Managing Effective Teams and Work Groups	Represents skills, abilities, or perspectives individuals need to build effective work groups	Brings out the best in people, participative management, forging synergy, building effective teams
Building and Maintaining Relationships	Represents skills, abilities, or perspectives individuals must demonstrate to build and keep effective relationships	Building relationships, putting people at ease, managing conflict, compassion and sensitivity, perspective-taking

(Continued)

Valuing Diversity and Difference	Represents skills, abilities, or perspectives that individuals use to effectively work with different kinds of people	Multi-cultural awareness, differences matter, valuing diversity, adapts to cultural differences, global awareness, cultural adaptability
Developing Others	Represents skills, abilities, or perspectives individuals need to develop others	Confronting problem employees; leading employees; selecting, developing, and accepting people; delegating; motivating; empowering
Communicating Effectively	Represents skills, abilities, or perspectives individuals need to effectively communicate with others	Communicating information and ideas, communicating effectively, listening, communication

Leading the Organization

Name	Description	Contains These Competencies
Managing Change	Represents skills, abilities, or perspectives individuals need to initiate and lead change	Change, recognizing the emotional impact of change, leading change, change management
Solving Problems and Making Decisions	Represents skills, abilities, or perspectives individuals should demonstrate to be effective problem solvers and decision makers	Getting information, making sense of it, sound judgment, problem solving/decision making, taking action, strategic thinking

Managing Politics and Influencing Others	Represents skills, abilities, or perspectives associated with influencing others and understanding organizational politics	Diplomacy, influencing, leadership, power, influence, influencing others, strategic influencing
Taking Risks and Innovating	Represents skills, abilities, or perspectives individuals need to seek and build new opportunities	Courage to take risks, risk taking, innovation, entrepreneurial, innovator
Setting Vision and Strategy	Represents skills, abilities, or perspectives associated with creating an organizational vision and setting the direction to manifest it	Planning and goal setting, strategic planning, vision
Managing the Work	Represents skills, abilities, or perspectives individuals should demonstrate to effectively manage work	Administrative/organizational ability, goal setting, set and achieve goals, management, results orientation, organizing
Enhancing Business Skills and Knowledge	Represents skills, abilities, or perspectives reflective of the general organizational knowledge that is needed to be effective	Customer/vendor relations, financial management, human resources, sales, international business knowledge
Understanding and Navigating the Organization	Represents skills, abilities, or perspectives associated with working within and across boundaries	Boundaries, working across boundaries, acting systemically, acting strategically

Leading Yourself

Name	Description	Contains These Competencies
Developing Adaptability	Represents skills, abilities, or perspectives individuals need to adjust to change	Openness to influence, flexibility, adaptability, embracing flexibility
Increasing Self-Awareness	Represents skills, abilities, or perspectives reflective of an individual's willingness to understand and improve self and seek feedback as a method for doing so	Self-awareness, awareness, increased self-awareness, seeks and uses feedback, self-development, open to criticism
Managing Yourself	Represents skills, abilities, or perspectives that can enable individuals to deal with pressure, set priorities, and balance conflicting interests	Career management, personal energy, balance between personal life and work, time management, coping with pressure and adversity, setting and obtaining goals
Increasing Your Capacity to Learn	Represents skills, abilities, or perspectives associated with learning from experience and openness to learning	Seeks opportunities to learn, learns from mistakes, learns from experience
Exhibiting Leadership Stature	Represents skills, abilities, or perspectives associated with positive attitudes, image, and inspiration	Executive image, leadership stature, personal style
Displaying Drive and Purpose	Represents skills, abilities, or perspectives indicative of the characteristics of perseverance, drive, and self-discipline	Energy, drive, ambition, committed to making a difference, doing whatever it takes
Demonstrating Ethics and Integrity	Represents skills, abilities, or perspectives reflective of trust, honesty, and integrity	Ethics, build and maintain credibility, credibility, ethics/culture, integrity, acts with integrity

CCL Leadership Competency Profile Tool

Table A.1

Number of Respondents: 0

	Competency Area	Importance	Skill	Difference		
Leading Others	Maintaining Effective Teams and Work Groups					
	Building and Maintaining Relationships					
	Valuing Diversity and Difference					
	Developing Others					
	Communicating Effectively					
Leading the Organization	Managing Change					
	Solving Problems and Making Decisions					
	Managing Politics and Influencing Others					
	Taking Risks and Innovating					
	Setting Vision and Strategy					
	Managing the Work					
	Enhancing Business Skills and Knowledge					
	Understanding and Navigating the Organization					
Leading Yourself	Demonstrating Ethics and Integrity					
	Displaying Drive and Purpose					
	Exhibiting Leadership Stature					
	Increasing Your Capacity to Learn					
	Managing Yourself					
	Increasing Self-Awareness					
	Developing Adaptability					

Legend:
Difference = Skill − Importance
+/− = The difference is 1.00 or more ("+" = Skill is higher; "−" = Skill is lower)

Rating Definitions:
1 = Not Important; 3 = Somewhat Important; 5 = Important; 7 = Critically Important

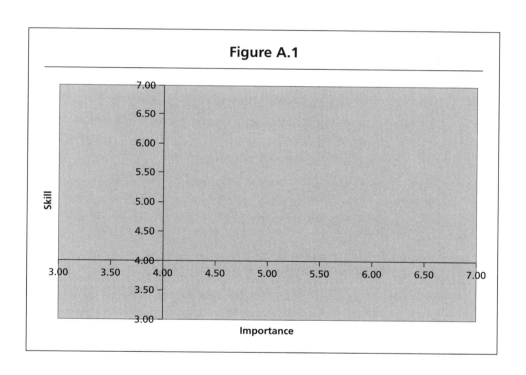

Figure A.1

Figure A.2

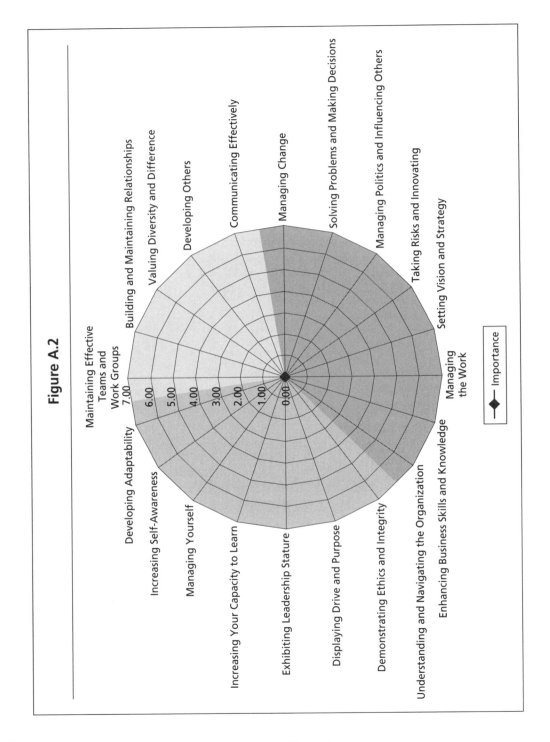

Maintaining Effective Teams and Work Groups

Building and Maintaining Relationships

Valuing Diversity and Difference

Developing Others

Communicating Effectively

Managing Change

Solving Problems and Making Decisions

Managing Politics and Influencing Others

Taking Risks and Innovating

Setting Vision and Strategy

Managing the Work

Understanding and Navigating the Organization

Enhancing Business Skills and Knowledge

Demonstrating Ethics and Integrity

Displaying Drive and Purpose

Exhibiting Leadership Stature

Increasing Your Capacity to Learn

Managing Yourself

Increasing Self-Awareness

Developing Adaptability

7.00 6.00 5.00 4.00 3.00 2.00 1.00 0.00

◆— Importance

REFERENCES

American Productivity and Quality Center. (2004). *Talent management: From competencies to organizational performance.* Houston, TX: Gulf.

Atwater, L. A., Waldman, D., Atwater, D., & Cartier, P. (2000). An upward feedback field experiment: Supervisors' cynicism, follow-up and commitment to subordinates. *Personnel Psychology, 53*(2), 275–297.

Block, P. (1991). *The empowered manager: Positive political skills at work.* San Francisco: Jossey-Bass.

Brutus, S., & Derayeh, M. (2002). Multisource assessment programs in organizations: An insider's perspective. *Human Resource Development Quarterly, 13*(2), 187–202.

Bunker, K., Kram, K., & Ting, S. (2002, December). The young and the clueless. *Harvard Business Review.*

Byham, W. C., Smith, A. B., & Paese, M. J. (2002). *Grow your own leaders: How to identify, develop, and retain leadership talent.* New York: FT Press.

Cherniss, C., & Adler, M. (2000). *Promoting emotional intelligence in organizations.* Alexandria, VA: American Society for Training & Development.

Corporate Leadership Council. (2001). *Voice of the leader: A quantitative analysis of leadership bench strength and development strategies.* Washington, DC: Corporate Executive Board.

Coy, P., & Ewing, J. (2007, April 9). Where are all the workers? *BusinessWeek,* 4029, 28–31.

Dalton, M. A. (1998). *Becoming a more versatile learner.* Greensboro, NC: Center for Creative Leadership.

Dalton, M. A., & Hollenbeck, G. P. (1996). *How to design an effective system for developing managers and executives.* Greensboro, NC: Center for Creative Leadership.

Fleenor, J., Taylor, S., & Chappelow, C. (2008). *Leveraging the impact of 360-degree feedback.* San Francisco: Pfeiffer.

Goleman, D. (1995). *Emotional intelligence: Why it can matter more than IQ.* New York: Bantam Books.

Guthrie, V. A., & King, S. N. (2004). Feedback-intensive programs. In C. D. McCauley & E. Van Velsor, *The Center for Creative Leadership handbook of leadership development* (2nd ed., pp. 25–57). San Francisco: Jossey-Bass.

Haapaniemi, P. (2002, October). Leading indicators: The development of executive leadership. *Chief Executive, 182*. Retrieved May 22, 2007, from http://findarticles.com/p/articles/mi_m4070/is_2002_Oct/ai_93207323/pg_2

Hannum, K. M., & Martineau, J. W. (2008). *Evaluating the impact of leadership development*. San Francisco: Pfeiffer.

Kirkpatrick, D. L. (1975). *Evaluating training programs*. Washington, DC: American Society for Training and Development.

Livers, A. B., & Caver, K. A. (2003). *Leading in black and white: Working across the racial divide in corporate America*. San Francisco: Jossey-Bass.

Livers, A. B., & Caver, K. A. (2004). Leader development across race. In C. D. McCauley & E. Van Velsor (Eds.), *The Center for Creative Leadership handbook of leadership development* (2nd ed., pp. 304–330). San Francisco: Jossey-Bass.

Lombardo, M. M., & Eichinger, R. W. (2002). *The leadership machine: Architecture to develop leaders for any future* (3rd ed.). Minneapolis, MN: Lominger.

Martineau, J. W. (2004). Evaluating the impact of leader development. In C. D. McCauley & E. Van Velsor, *The Center for Creative Leadership handbook of leadership development* (2nd ed., pp. 234–267). San Francisco: Jossey-Bass.

McCall, M. W., Jr., Lombardo, M. M., & Morrison, A. M. (1988). *The lessons of experience: How successful executives develop on the job*. Lexington, MA: Lexington Books.

McCauley, C. D. (2006). *Developmental assignments: Creating learning experiences without changing jobs*. Greensboro, NC: Center for Creative Leadership.

McCauley, C. D., & Douglas, C. A. (2004). Developmental relationships. In C. D. McCauley & E. Van Velsor, *The Center for Creative Leadership handbook of leadership development* (2nd ed., pp. 85–115). San Francisco: Jossey-Bass.

McCauley, C. D., & Van Velsor, E. (2004). *The Center for Creative Leadership handbook of leadership development* (2nd ed.). San Francisco: Jossey-Bass.

Michaels, E., Handfield-Jones, H., & Axelrod, B. (2001). *The war for talent*. Boston: Harvard Business School Press.

Smither, J. W., London, M., & Richmond, K. R. (2005). The relationship between leaders' personality and their reactions to and use of multi-source feedback. *Group and Organization Management, 30*(2), 181–210.

Towers Perrin. (2002). *The Towers Perrin talent report: How leading organizations manage talent*. Retrieved May 9, 2007, from www.towersperrin.com/tp/getwebcachedoc?webc=HRS/USA/2002/200210/TM_Best_Practices.pdf.

Van Velsor, E., Moxley, R. S., & Bunker, K. A. (2004). The leader development process. In C. D. McCauley & E. Van Velsor, *The Center for Creative Leadership handbook of leadership development* (2nd ed., pp. 204–233). San Francisco: Jossey-Bass.

Walker, A. G., & Smither, J. W. (1999). A five-year study of upward feedback: What managers do with their results matters. *Personnel Psychology, 52*(2), 393–423.

Business Strategy/Organizational Needs

Berke, D. (2002). Finding success at succession. *Leadership in Action, 22*(5), 20–21.

Berke, D. (2005). *Succession planning and management: A guide to organizational systems and practices.* Greensboro, NC: Center for Creative Leadership.

Chambers, E. G., Foulon, M., Handfield-Jones, H., Hankin, S. H., & Michaels, E. G., III. (1998). The war for talent. *The McKinsey Quarterly, 3,* 44–57.

Charan, R. (2005). Ending the CEO succession crisis. *Harvard Business Review, 83*(2), 72–81.

Charan, R., Drotter, S., & Noel, J. (2001). *Leadership pipeline: How to build the leadership-powered company.* San Francisco: Jossey-Bass.

Charan, R., & Useem, J. (2002, November 18). The five pitfalls of CEO succession. *Fortune, 146,* 78.

Clark, L. A., & Lyness, K. S. (1991). Succession planning as a strategic activity at Citicorp. In L. W. Foster (Ed.), *Advances in applied business strategy* (Vol. 2, pp. 205–224). Greenwich, CT: JAI Press.

Cohn, J. M., Khurana, R., & Reeves, L. (2005). Growing talent as if your business depended on it. *Harvard Business Review, 83*(10), 63–70.

Conger, J. A., & Nadler, D. A. (2004). When CEOs step up to fail. *MIT Sloan Management Review, 45*(3), 50–56.

Corporate Leadership Council. (2003). *High-impact succession management: From succession planning to strategic executive talent management.* Washington, DC: Author.

Downey, D., March, T., & Berkman, A. (2001). *Assimilating new leaders: The key to executive retention.* New York: AMACOM.

Eastman, L. J. (1995). *Succession planning: An annotated bibliography and summary of commonly reported organizational practices.* Greensboro, NC: Center for Creative Leadership.

Fitz-enz, J. (2000). *The ROI of human capital: Measuring the economic value of employee performance.* New York: AMACOM.

Frank, F. D., Finnegan, R. P., & Taylor, C. R. (2004). The race for talent: Retaining and engaging workers in the 21st century. *Human Resource Planning, 27*(3), 12–25.

Fulmer, R. M., & Conger, J. A. (2004). *Growing your company's leaders: How great organizations use succession management to sustain competitive advantage.* New York: AMACOM.

Fulmer, R. M., & Goldsmith, M. (2001). *The leadership investment: How the world's best organizations gain strategic advantage through leadership development.* New York: AMACOM.

Grigoryev, P. (2006). Hiring by competency models. *Journal for Quality & Participation, 29*(4), 16–18.

Hall, D. (1995). Executive careers and learning: Aligning selection, strategy, and development. *Human Resource Planning, 18*(2), 14–23.

Ingham, J. (2006). Closing the talent management gap. *Strategic HR Review, 5*(3), 20–23.

Jenkins, M. (2006). Managing talent is a burning issue in Asia. *Leadership in Action, 26*(5), 20–22.

Karaevli, A., & Hall, D. T. (2003). Growing leaders for turbulent times: Is succession planning up to the challenge? *Organizational Dynamics, 32*(1), 62–79.

Khurana, R. (2001). Finding the right CEO: Why boards often make poor choices. *MIT Sloan Management Review, 43*(1), 91–95.

Laff, M. (2006). Talent management: From hire to retire. *T+D, 60*(11), 42–48.

Leonard, H. S., & Goff, N. (2003). Leadership development as an intervention for organizational transformation. *Consulting Psychology Journal, 55*, 58–67.

Lewis, B. O. (2003, January). Organizational assessments: Aligning learning with strategic directions. *Chief Learning Officer.* Retrieved June 15, 2007, from www.CLO.com.

Lewis, R. E., & Heckman, R. J. (2006). Talent management: A critical review. *Human Resource Management Review, 16*(2), 139–154.

Lombardo, M. M., & Eichinger, R. W. (2000). High potentials as high learners. *Human Resource Management, 39*(4), 321–329.

McCall, M. W., Jr. (1998). *High flyers: Developing the next generation of leaders.* Boston: Harvard Business School Press.

McCauley, C., & Wakefield, M. (2006). Talent management in the 21st century: Help your company find, develop, and keep its strongest workers. *Journal for Quality & Participation, 29*(4), 4–7.

Mihm, J. C. (2003, October 1). *Human capital: Succession management is critical driver of organizational transformation.* United States General Accounting Office. Retrieved June 8, 2007, from www.gao.gov/new.items/d04127t.pdf.

Ready, D. A., & Conger, J. A. (2007). Make your company a talent factory. *Harvard Business Review, 85*(6), 68–77.

Robinson, G. S., & Wick, C. W. (1992). Executive development that makes a business difference. *Human Resource Planning, 15*(5), 63–76.

Rothwell, W. J. (2001). *Effective succession planning: Ensuring leadership continuity and building talent from within* (2nd ed.). New York: AMACOM.

Ruderman, M. N., & Ohlott, P. J. (1990). *Traps and pitfalls in the judgment of executive potential.* Greensboro, NC: Center for Creative Leadership.

Seibert, K. W., Hall, D. T., & Kram, K. (1995). Strengthening the weak link in strategic executive development: Integrating individual development and global business strategy. *Human Resource Management, 34,* 529–547.

Sessa, V. I., Kaiser, R., Taylor, J. K., & Campbell, R. J. (1998). *Executive selection: A research report on what works and what doesn't.* Greensboro, NC: Center for Creative Leadership.

Tumolo, B., & Tumolo, M. (2004). *Leveraging the new human capital.* Palo Alto, CA: Davies-Black.

Uren, L. (2007). From talent compliance to talent commitment. *Strategic HR Review, 6*(3), 32–35.

Wiersema, M. (2002). Holes at the top: Why CEO firings backfire. *Harvard Business Review, 80*(12), 70–77.

Zhang, Y., & Rajagopalan, N. (2004). When the known devil is better than an unknown god: An empirical study of the antecedents and consequences of relay CEO successions. *Academy of Management Journal, 47,* 483–500.

Development Strategies

Allinson, C. W., & Hayes, J. (1988). The learning styles questionnaire: An alternative to Kolb's inventory? *Journal of Management Studies, 25*(3), 269–281.

Andrew, M. (2003, December). Winning strategies for leadership development. *Chief Learning Officer.* Retrieved June 8, 2007, from www.clomedia.com/content/templates/.

Barbian, J. (2001). The future training room. *Training, 38*(9), 40–45.

Brennan, J. (2003). Reality check: The new learner needs. *Training & Development, 57*(5), 23–25.

Browning, H., & Van Velsor, E. (1999). *Three keys to development: Defining and meeting your leadership challenges.* Greensboro, NC: Center for Creative Leadership.

Bunker, K. A., & Webb, A. D. (1992). *Learning how to learn from experience: Impact of stress and coping.* Greensboro, NC: Center for Creative Leadership.

Caudron, S. (2000). Learners speak out. *Training & Development, 54*(4), 52–57.

Charan, R., Drotter, S., & Noel, J. (2000). *The leadership pipeline: How to build the leadership powered company.* San Francisco: Jossey-Bass.

Corporate Leadership Council. (2001). *The leadership imperative: Strategies for increasing leadership bench strength.* Washington, DC: Author.

Corporate Leadership Council. (2001). *Voice of the leader: A quantitative analysis of leadership bench strength and development strategies.* Washington, DC: Author.

Corporate Leadership Council. (2003). *Hallmarks of leadership success: Strategies for improving leadership quality and executive readiness.* Washington, DC: Author.

Douglas, C. A. (2003). *Key events and lessons for managers in a diverse workforce: A report on research and findings*. Greensboro, NC: Center for Creative Leadership.

Ernst, C., & Martin, A. (2007). Experience counts: Learning lessons from key events. *Leadership in Action, 26*(6), 3–7.

Farrell, J. N. (2000). Long live c-learning. *Training & Development, 54*(9), 43–46.

Giber, D., Carter, L. L., & Goldsmith, M. (Eds.). (2000). *Linkage Inc.'s best practices in leadership development handbook: Case studies, instruments, training*. San Francisco: Jossey-Bass.

Hayes, J., & Allinson, C. W. (1988). Cultural differences in the learning styles of managers. *Management International Review, 23*(3), 75–80.

Lindsey, E. H., Homes, V., & McCall, M. W., Jr. (1987). *Key events in executives' lives*. Greensboro, NC: Center for Creative Leadership.

Lombardo, M. M., & Eichinger, R. W. (1989). *Eighty-eight assignments for development in place*. Greensboro, NC: Center for Creative Leadership.

Marquardt, M. J. (1999). *Action learning in action*. Palo Alto, CA: Davies-Black.

Marquardt, M. J. (2004). *Action learning: Solving problems and building leaders in real time*. Palo Alto, CA: Davies-Black.

Martineau, J., & Johnson, E. (2001). *Preparing for development: Making the most of formal leadership programs*. Greensboro, NC: Center for Creative Leadership.

Martineau, J. W., & Steed, J. L. (2001). Follow up: A valuable tool in leadership development. *Leadership in Action, 21*(1), 1–6.

McCall, M. W., Jr. (1998). *High flyers: Developing the next generation of leaders*. Boston: Harvard Business School Press.

McCauley, C. D. (2006). *Developmental assignments: Creating learning experiences without changing jobs*. Greensboro, NC: Center for Creative Leadership.

McCauley, C. D., & Brutus, S. (1998). *Management development through job experiences: An annotated bibliography*. Greensboro, NC: Center for Creative Leadership.

McCauley, C. D., & Van Velsor, E. (Eds.). (2004). *The Center for Creative Leadership handbook of leadership development* (2nd ed.). San Francisco: Jossey-Bass.

Rossett, A., & Sheldon, K. (2001). *Beyond the podium: Delivering training and performance to a digital world*. San Francisco: Pfeiffer.

Ukens, L. L. (Ed.). (2001). *What smart trainers know: The secrets of success from the world's foremost experts*. San Francisco: Pfeiffer.

Gaps, Skills, and Target Populations

Atwater, L. E., Ostroff, C., Yammarino, F. J., & Fleenor, J. W. (1998). Self-other agreement: Does it really matter? *Personnel Psychology, 51*(3), 577–598.

Brannick, M. T., Salas, E., & Prince, C. (Eds.). (1997). *Team performance assessment and measurement: Theory, methods, and applications*. Mahwah, NJ: Lawrence Erlbaum Associates.

Brutus, S., Fleenor, J. W., & London, M. (1998). Does 360-degree feedback work in different industries? A between-industry comparison of the reliability and validity of multi-source performance ratings. *Journal of Management Development, 17*(3), 177–190.

Brutus, S., Fleenor, J. W., & McCauley, C. D. (1999). Demographic and personality predictors of congruence in multi-source ratings. *Journal of Management Development, 18*(5), 417–435.

Brutus, S., & Kelly-Radford, L. (1998). Receptivity to feedback. *Leadership in Action, 18*(5), 8–10.

Craig, S. B., & Hannum, K. (2006). Research update: 360-degree performance assessment. *Consulting Psychology Journal: Practice and Research, 58*(2), 117–124.

Dalton, M. A. (1998). Using 360-degree feedback successfully. *Leadership in Action, 18*(1), 2–11.

DeNisi, A. S., & Kluger, A. N. (2000). Feedback effectiveness: Can 360-degree appraisals be improved? *Academy of Management Executive, 14*(1), 129–139.

Fleenor, J. W., & Prince, J. M. (1997). *Using 360-degree feedback in organizations: An annotated bibliography.* Greensboro, NC: Center for Creative Leadership.

Gentry, W. A., & Leslie, J. B. (2007). Competencies for leadership development: What's hot and what's not when assessing leadership—implications for organization development. *Organization Development Journal, 25*(1), 37–46.

Goldsmith, M. (2003). Evaluating individual performance? *New Zealand Management, 50*(3), 34–37.

Hannum, K. (2003). Best practices: Choosing the right methods for evaluation. *Leadership in Action, 23*(6), 14–19.

Holton, E. F., Bates, R. A., & Naquin, S. S. (2000). Large-scale performance-driven training needs assessment: A case study. *Public Personnel Management, 29*(2), 249–267.

Leslie, J. B., & Fleenor, J. W. (1998). *Feedback to managers: A review and comparison of multi-rater instruments for management development* (3rd ed.). Greensboro, NC: Center for Creative Leadership.

Leslie, J. B., Penny, J., & Suzuki, M. (2002). *Assessing individual managerial skill across cultures: The influence of language and rating source on 360-degree feedback.* Presented at Society for Industrial & Organizational Psychology in April 2002.

Leslie, J. B., Van Velsor, E., & Fleenor, J. W. (1997). *Choosing 360: A guide to evaluating multi-rater feedback instruments for management development.* Greensboro, NC: Center for Creative Leadership.

London, M., Smither, J. W., & Adsit, D. J. (1997). Accountability: The Achilles' heel of multisource feedback. *Group & Organization Management, 22*(2), 162–184.

Ludeman, K. (2000). How to conduct self-directed 360. *Training & Development, 54*(6), 44–47.

Martineau, J. (2003). Laying the groundwork: First steps in evaluating leadership development. *Leadership in Action, 23*(6), 3–8.

Morical, K. E. (1999). A product review: 360 assessments. *Training & Development, 53*(4), 43–47.

Penny, J. (2001). Differential item functioning in an international 360-assessment: Evidence of gender stereotype, environmental complexity, and organizational contingency. *European Journal of Work and Organizational Psychology, 10*(3), 245–271.

Smither, J. W., London, M., Reilly, R. R., Flautt, R., Vargas, Y., & Kucine, I. (2004). Discussing multisource feedback with raters and performance improvement. *Journal of Management Development, 23*(5), 456–468.

Tornow, W. W., London, M., & CCL Associates. (1998). *Maximizing the value of 360-degree feedback: A process for successful individual and organizational development.* San Francisco: Jossey-Bass.

Tornow, W. W., & Pinto, P. R. (1976). The development of a managerial job taxonomy: A system for describing, classifying, and evaluating executive positions. *Journal of Applied Psychology, 61*(4), 410–418.

Van Velsor, E., Leslie, J. B., & Fleenor, J. W. (1997). *Choosing 360: A guide to evaluating multi-rater feedback instruments for management development.* Greensboro, NC: Center for Creative Leadership.

Yammarino, F. J., & Atwater, L. E. (1997). Do managers see themselves as others see them? Implications of self-other rating agreement for human resources management. *Organizational Dynamics, 25*(4), 35–44.

Zaccaro, S. J. (2001). *The nature of executive leadership: A conceptual and empirical analysis of success.* Washington, DC: American Psychological Association.

Implementation

Aaltonen, P., & Ikävalko, H. (2002). Implementing strategies successfully. *Integrated Manufacturing Systems, 13*(6), 415–418.

AICPA. (2005). *Preparing for transition: The state of succession planning and how to handle transition in your firm* (white paper). American Institute of Certified Public Accountants. Retrieved June 8, 2007, from http://pcps.aicpa.org/NR/rdonlyres/D1C10A9F-6592-4315-B686-FD27CB55B6BA/0/PCPSWhitePaper_SuccPlan.pdf.

Aldrich, C. (2003). Using leadership to implement leadership. *T+D, 57*(5), 94–100.

Bourne, M., Mill, J., Wilcox, M., Neely, A., & Platts, K. (2000). Designing, implementing, and updating performance measurement systems. *International Journal of Operations & Production Management, 20*(7), 754–771.

Cacioppe, R. (1998). An integrated model and approach for the design of effective leadership development programs. *Leadership & Organization Development Journal, 19*(1), 44–53.

Cheng, M. I., Dainty, A., & Moore, D. (2007). Implementing a new performance management system within a project-based organization: A case study. *International Journal of Productivity and Performance Management, 56*(1), 60–75. Retrieved June 20, 2007, from www.emeraldinsight.com/Insight/.

Dixon, N. M. (1995). A practical model for organizational learning. *Issues & Observations, 15*(2), 1–4.

Eichinger, R. W., & Lombardo, M. M. (1990). *Twenty-two ways to develop leadership in staff managers*. Greensboro, NC: Center for Creative Leadership.

Green, M. (2005). 10 tips for creating a public sector leadership development program. *Government Finance Review, 21*(3), 58–60.

Griffin, M. A., Rafferty, A. E., & Mason, C. M. (2004). Who started this? Investigating different sources of organizational change. *Journal of Business & Psychology, 18*(4), 555–570.

Hughes, R., & Beatty, K. (2005). Five steps to leading strategically. *T&D, 59*(12), 46–48.

Matheny, J. A. (1998). Organizational therapy: Relating a psychotherapeutic model of planned personal change to planned organizational change. *Journal of Managerial Psychology, 13*(5/6), 394–405.

McGee, L. (2004). How to . . . implement a succession plan. *People Management, 10*(23), 48–49.

Mourier, P., & Smith, M. R. (2001). *Conquering organizational change: How to succeed where most companies fail*. Atlanta, GA: CEP Press.

Okumus, F. (2003). A framework to implement strategies in organizations. *Management Decision, 41*(9), 871–882.

Pulley, M. L. (1997). Leading resilient organizations. *Leadership in Action, 17*(4), 1–5.

Reeves, D. (2007). Closing the implementation. *Educational Leadership, 64*(6), 85–86.

Rogers, R. E., & Fong, J. Y. (2000). *Organizational assessment: Diagnosis and intervention*. Amherst, MA: HRD Press.

Villanueva, T. (2003). Back to basics. *HRMagazine, 48*(5), 95–99.

Leadership Competencies

Barner, R. (2000). Five steps to leadership competencies. *Training & Development, 54*(3), 47–51.

Burnett, M., & Dutsch, J. V. (2006). Competency-based training and assessment center: Strategies, technology, process, and issues. *Advances in Developing Human Resources, 8*(2), 141–143.

Conger, J. A., & Ready, D. A. (2004). Rethinking leadership competencies. *Leader to Leader, 32*, 41–47.

Davis, P., Naughton, J., & Rothwell, W. (2004). New roles and new competencies for the profession. *T+D, 58*(4), 26–36.

Dunn, J., & Mitchell, K. (1979). Sample competency-based modularized instructional systems and systems components. *Instructional management systems: Components review*. Ithaca, NY: Cornell University, Institute for Occupational Education.

Eyde, L. D., Gregory, D. J., Muldrow, T. W., & Mergen, P. K. (1999). *High-performance leaders, a competency model*. Washington, DC: U.S. Office of Employment Management, Employment Service, Personnel Resources and Development Center.

Green, P. C. (1999). *Building robust competencies*. San Francisco: Jossey-Bass.

Hollenbeck, G. P., McCall, M. W., & Silzer, R. F. (2006). Leadership competency models. *Leadership Quarterly, 17*(4), 398–413.

Holton, E. F., & Naquin, S. S. (Eds.). (2000). *Developing high-performance leadership competency, advances in developing human resources.* San Francisco: Berrett-Koehler.

Kaplan, R. E. (1999). *Internalizing strengths: An overlooked way of overcoming weaknesses in managers.* Greensboro, NC: Center for Creative Leadership.

Le Deist, F. D., Delamare, F., & Winterton, J. (2005). What is competence? *Journal of Human Resource Development International, 8*(1), 27–46.

Lombardo, M. M., & Eichinger, R. W. (2002). *For your improvement™: A development and coaching guide* (3rd ed.). Minneapolis, MN: Lominger.

Lucia, A. D., & Lepsinger, R. (1999). *The art and science of competency models: Pinpointing critical success factors in organizations.* San Francisco: Jossey-Bass.

Montier, R., Alai, D., & Kramer, D. (2006). Competency models develop top performance. *T+D, 60*(7), 47–50.

Naquin, S. S., & Holton, E. F., III. (2006). Leadership and managerial competency models: A simplified process and resulting model. *Developing Human Resources, 8*(2), 144–165.

Palus, C. J., & Horth, D. M. (2002). *The leader's edge: Six creative competencies for navigating complex challenges.* San Francisco: Jossey-Bass.

Rosier, R. (1994–1997). *Competency model handbook, Volumes 1–4.* Lexington, MA: Linkage, Inc.

Rothwell, W., & Wellins, R. (2004). Mapping your future: Putting new competencies to work for you. *T+D, 58*(5), 94–101.

Spencer, L. M., Jr., & Spencer, S. M. (1993). *Competence at work: Models for superior performance.* Hoboken, NJ: John Wiley & Sons.

Zaccaro, S. J. (2001). *The nature of executive leadership: A conceptual and empirical analysis of success.* Washington, DC: American Psychological Association.

Ongoing Evaluation

Brinkerhoff, R. O. (2003). *The success case method: Find out quickly what's working and what's not.* San Francisco: Berrett-Koehler.

Frierson, H. T. (2003). The importance of increasing the numbers of individuals of color to enhance cultural responsiveness in program evaluation. In C. C. Yeakey & R. Henderson (Eds.), *Surrounding all odds: Education, opportunity, and society in the new millennium.* Greenwich, CT: Information Age.

Grove, J., Kibel, B., & Haas, T. (2005). *EvaluLEAD: A guide for shaping and evaluating leadership development programs.* W. K. Kellogg Foundation and Public Health Institute. Retrieved May 1, 2007, from www.wkkf.org/pubs/tools/evaluation/evalulead4_00447_03740.pdf.

Gutiérrez, M., & Stowell, B. (2004). *Next generation leadership program: Final assessment report.* Philadelphia: OMG Center for Collaborative Learning.

Hannum, K. M., Martineau, J. W., & Reinelt, C. (Eds.). (2007). *The handbook of leadership development evaluation.* San Francisco: Jossey-Bass.

Hodges, T. K. (2001). *Linking learning and performance: A practical guide to measuring learning and on-the-job application.* Boston: Butterworth-Heinemann.

Hood, S. (2001). *New look at an old question: The cultural context of educational evaluation: The role of minority evaluation professionals.* Arlington, VA: National Science Foundation.

Hopson, R. K. (2003). *Overview of multicultural and culturally competent program evaluation: Issues, challenges, and opportunities.* Woodland Hills, CA: The California Endowment.

Kirkpatrick, D. L. (1998). *Another look at evaluating training programs: Fifty articles from* Training & Development *and* Technical Training *magazines cover the essentials of evaluation and return-on-investment.* Alexandria, VA: American Society for Training and Development.

Kirkpatrick, D. L. (1998). *Evaluating training programs: The four levels* (2nd ed.). San Francisco: Berrett-Koehler.

Leslie, J. B., & Fleenor, J. W. (1998). *Feedback to managers: A review and comparison of multi-rater instruments for management development.* Greensboro, NC: Center for Creative Leadership.

Leslie, J. B., Van Velsor, E., & Fleenor, J. W. (1997). *Choosing 360: A guide to evaluating multi-rater feedback instruments for management development.* Greensboro, NC: Center for Creative Leadership.

Martineau, J. (2004). Laying the groundwork: First steps in evaluating leadership development. *Leadership in Action, 23*(6), 3–8.

McDavid, J. C., & Hawthorn, L. R. L. (2006). *Program evaluation and performance measurement.* Thousand Oaks, CA: Sage.

Michalski, G. V., & Cousins, J. B. (2000). Differences in stakeholder perceptions about training evaluation: A concept mapping/pattern matching investigation. *Evaluation and Programme Planning, 23*(2), 211–230.

Michalski, G. V., & Cousins, J. B. (2001). Multiple perspectives on training evaluation: Probing stakeholder perceptions in a global network development firm. *American Journal of Evaluation, 22*(1), 37–53.

Packard Foundation Population Program and the Bill and Melinda Gates Foundation Global Health Program. (2003). *Guide to evaluating leadership development programs.* Seattle, WA: Evaluation Forum.

Phillips, J. (2003). *Return on investment in training and performance improvement programs* (2nd ed.). Woburn, MA: Butterworth-Heinemann.

Phillips, J., & Phillips, P. (2005). *ROI at work: Best-practice case studies from the real world.* Alexandria, VA: ASTD Press.

Phillips, J., Phillips, P., & Hodges, T. (2004). *Make training evaluation work.* Alexandria, VA: ASTD Press.

Phillips, J., & Schmidt, L. (2004). *The leadership scorecard.* Woburn, MA: Butterworth-Heinemann.

Phillips, J., Stone, R., & Phillips, P. (2001). *The human resources scorecard: Measuring the return on investment.* Woburn, MA: Butterworth-Heinemann.

Phillips, P. (2002). *The bottom line on ROI.* Atlanta, GA: Center for Effective Performance.

Posavac, E. J., & Carey, R. G. (2006). *Program evaluation: Methods and case studies* (7th ed.). Upper Saddle River, NJ: Prentice Hall.

Pratt, C., McGuigan, W., & Katzev, A. (2000). Measuring program outcomes: Using retrospective pretest methodology. *American Journal of Evaluation, 21*(3), 341–349.

Preskill, H., & Russ-Eft, D. (2001). A system model for evaluating learning performance. In D. H. Redmann (Ed.), *Academy of Human Resource Development: Defining the cutting edge.* Baton Rouge, LA: Academy of Human Resource Development.

Preskill, H., & Russ-Eft, D. (2003). A framework for reframing HRD evaluation practice and research. In A. M. Gilley, L. Bierema, & J. Callahan (Eds.), *Critical issues in HRD.* Cambridge, MA: Perseus.

Preskill, H., & Russ-Eft, D. (2005). *Building evaluation capacity: 72 activities for teaching and training.* Thousand Oaks, CA: Sage.

Preskill, H., & Torres, R. T. (1999). *Evaluative inquiry for learning in organizations.* Thousand Oaks, CA: Sage.

Rohs, F. R. (1999). Response shift bias: A problem in evaluating leadership development with self-report pretest-posttest measures. *Journal of Agricultural Education, 40*(4), 28–37.

Rohs, F. R. (2002). Improving the evaluation of leadership programs: Control response shift. *Journal of Leadership Education, 1,* 50–61.

Rohs, F. R., & Langone, C. A. (1997). Increased accuracy in measuring leadership impacts. *Journal of Leadership Studies, 4*(1), 150–158.

Russ-Eft, D., Atwood, R., & Egherman, T. (2002). Use and non-use of evaluation results: A case study of environmental influences in private sector. *American Journal of Evaluation, 23,* 19–31.

Russ-Eft, D., & Hoover, A. L. (2002). Experimental and quasi-experimental designs. In R. A. Swanson & E. F. Holton (Eds.), *Research in organizations: Foundations in methods of inquiry.* San Francisco: Berrett-Koehler.

Russ-Eft, D., & Preskill, H. (2001). *Evaluation in organizations: A systematic approach to enhance learning, performance, and change.* Cambridge, MA: Perseus.

Russ-Eft, D., & Preskill, H. (2003). A framework for reframing HRD evaluation, practice, and research. In A. M. Gilley, J. L. Callahan, & L. L. Bierema (Eds.), *Critical issues in HRD: A new agenda for the twenty-first century.* Cambridge, MA: Perseus.

Russ-Eft, D., & Preskill, H. (2005). In search of the holy grail: Return on investment evaluation in human resource development. *Advances in Developing Human Resources, 7*(1), 71–85.

Sogunro, O. A. (1997). Impact of training on leadership development. *Evaluation Review, 21*(6), 713–737.

Torres, R. T., Preskill, H., & Piontek, M. (2005). *Evaluation strategies for communicating and reporting: Enhancing learning in organizations* (2nd ed.). Thousand Oaks, CA: Sage.

W. K. Kellogg Foundation and Development Guild/DDI. (2002). *Evaluating outcomes and impacts: A scan of 55 leadership development programs.* Battle Creek, MI: W. K. Kellogg Foundation.

INDEX

A

Abrasive Technology, 26, 34
ACS (assessment, challenge, support) model
    business/organizational assessment component of, 14–31, 33–35
    CCL competency wheel component of, 36t–40
    development strategies component of, 53–73
    illustrated diagram of, 6*fig*
    implementation component of, 75–86
    organizational challenges component of, 27t–31
    over view of, 6–7
    support component of, 55, 83–86
    See also DLT (Developing Leadership Talent)
Adversaries stakeholders, 83*e*, 84*fig*
Allies stakeholders, 84*fig*, 85*e*
American Productivity and Quality Center (APQC), 2–3
Apple Computer, 25, 26
Associates stakeholders, 84*fig*, 85*e*
Atwater, D., 71
Atwater, L. A., 71
Axelrod, B., 1

B

Behavior. *See* Leadership behavior
Berayeh, M., 72
Block, P., 84
Brutus, S., 72
Bunker, K. A., 50, 55, 57
Business challenges
    assessment considerations of, 14–15
    implications for leaders and organizations, 27t–31
Business Strategy/Need Assessment Matrix, 20*e*
Business Strategy/Need Assessment Worksheet, 21*e*–22*e*
Business/organizational assessment
    Business Strategy/Need Assessment Matrix for, 20*e*
    Business Strategy/Need Assessment Worksheet for, 21*e*–22*e*
    checklist for, 23
    implications for leadership, 25–31
    Key Leader Focus-Group Session used for, 19*e*
    leadership competencies aligned with, 33–35
    organizational challenges to consider in, 14–15
    survey or interview guide for, 16*e*–17*e*
Byham, W. C., 50

C

D

ongoing evaluation approach by, 88–105

overview of, 6–9

See also ACS (assessment, challenge, support) model; CCL (Center for Creative Leadership)

DLT Planning Worksheet (Proposal Outline), 80*e*

Douglas, C. A., 66

E

Eichinger, R. W., 50

Emotional intelligence

description and research on, 55–56

DLT approach and issue of, 56–57

Employees

development job assignments and, 59–67*e*

new hires, high potentials, and solid performers, 49–51

See also Leadership development

Evaluating the Impact of Leadership Development (Martineau & Hannum), 88

Evaluation

checklist for ongoing, 105

data-collection methods used for, 97, 100

determining questions used in, 94, 98*e*–99*e*

determining resources for, 94

DLT phases of, 88–105

establishing types of impact and time frame, 89

Evaluation Expectations Worksheet, 94, 95*e*–96*e*

Evaluation Purpose Definition Worksheet, 89, 92*e*–93*e*

Evaluation Questions Worksheet, 98*e*–99*e*

guidelines for, 100–101, 102*e*–103*e*

integration with initiative design approach to, 87

Kirkpatrick's four-level model of, 88

organizational learning approach to, 87

participatory approach to, 87

three principles of ongoing and effective, 87

Using Evaluation Findings Checklist, 104*e*

Evaluation phases

designing and conducting the evaluation, 100–101, 102*e*–103*e*

using evaluation findings, 101–105, 104*e*

focusing the evaluation, 89–100

Evaluation-Assessment Make the Case, 81

Ewing, J., 1

F

Feedback

Feedback-Intensive Program Activities, 70*t*

management encouragement of, 66

multi-rater feedback instruments used for, 68–69, 70*t*

See also 360-degree feedback

Feedback-Intensive Program Activities, 70*t*

Fleenor, J., 72

G

Gap analysis

checklist on gaps, skills, and target populations, 51–52

defining the current state, 44–46

defining the future state, 46–47*e*

definition of, 43

Gaps, Skills, and Target Populations Worksheet, 47*e*

identifying target populations, 49–51

illustrated diagram of DLT, 44*fig*

ABOUT THE AUTHORS

David Berke is a principal at Lorsch, Berke and Associates, a firm that specializes in succession, talent management, and leadership development. He has worked with organizations such as Google, Hewlett Packard, and Siemens, as well as nonprofits and government agencies. He has worked in the United States, Asia, and Europe.

David was previously a senior faculty member at the Center for Creative Leadership (CCL), focusing on assessment, design, and implementation of customer-specific initiatives. Before joining CCL, David designed and led management, leadership, and organization development activities in several industries, including aerospace, health care, and public utilities. This included a large-scale culture change effort at a Fortune 200 company.

In addition to this book, David has written *Succession Planning and Management: A Guide to Organizational Systems and Practices,* as well as several articles on succession planning and talent management.

David holds an M.B.A. from the University of Southern California, an M.A. in English literature from the State University of New York at Stony Brook, and a B.A. in English literature from the University of California at Santa Cruz.

Michael E. Kossler is a lead senior enterprise associate at CCL. In this role, he works with global clients to assess their organizations' leadership development needs and then to design and implement custom solutions. Prior to assuming his current role, Mike was manager, custom solutions at CCL's European campus based in Brussels. He also served as the project manager for CCL's research on geographically dispersed teams.

Mike has collaborated with a variety of international organizations, including Alstom, Citigroup, Novartis, Siemens, and Xerox. He frequently works with executive-level teams on issues of organizational effectiveness, change management, and business strategy development. Mike holds an M.A. in communications from the University of Akron and an M.M. in organization development from Aquinas College. He has completed postgraduate work at both the Indianapolis Gestalt Institute and the Gestalt Institute of Cleveland.

Michael Wakefield is a senior program associate at CCL. He serves as the manager of trainer development and designs and delivers customized, client-specific programs. He also trains in several of CCL's open-enrollment programs, including the Leadership Development Program, Coaching for Development, and Building Resiliency: Leading in the Face of Change. He is the co-author of *Leading with Authenticity in Times of Change, Building Resiliency,* and has written or contributed to other publications as well.

Michael has held a variety of training and counseling roles, including the development and delivery of cross-cultural assimilation training for Peace Corps trainers and volunteers in Belize, Central America. Both his bachelor's and master's degrees are in psychology. Michael is certified by the Society for Human Resource Management as a Senior Professional in Human Resources, and he is licensed as a professional counselor.

Pfeiffer Publications Guide

This guide is designed to familiarize you with the various types of Pfeiffer publications. The formats section describes the various types of products that we publish; the methodologies section describes the many different ways that content might be provided within a product. We also provide a list of the topic areas in which we publish.

FORMATS

In addition to its extensive book-publishing program, Pfeiffer offers content in an array of formats, from fieldbooks for the practitioner to complete, ready-to-use training packages that support group learning.

FIELDBOOK Designed to provide information and guidance to practitioners in the midst of action. Most fieldbooks are companions to another, sometimes earlier, work, from which its ideas are derived; the fieldbook makes practical what was theoretical in the original text. Fieldbooks can certainly be read from cover to cover. More likely, though, you'll find yourself bouncing around following a particular theme, or dipping in as the mood, and the situation, dictate.

HANDBOOK A contributed volume of work on a single topic, comprising an eclectic mix of ideas, case studies, and best practices sourced by practitioners and experts in the field.

An editor or team of editors usually is appointed to seek out contributors and to evaluate content for relevance to the topic. Think of a handbook not as a ready-to-eat meal, but as a cookbook of ingredients that enables you to create the most fitting experience for the occasion.

RESOURCE Materials designed to support group learning. They come in many forms: a complete, ready-to-use exercise (such as a game); a comprehensive resource on one topic (such as conflict management) containing a variety of methods and approaches; or a collection of like-minded activities (such as icebreakers) on multiple subjects and situations.

TRAINING PACKAGE An entire, ready-to-use learning program that focuses on a particular topic or skill. All packages comprise a guide for the facilitator/trainer and a workbook for the participants. Some packages are supported with additional media—such as video—or learning aids, instruments, or other devices to help participants understand concepts or practice and develop skills.

- *Facilitator/trainer's guide* Contains an introduction to the program, advice on how to organize and facilitate the learning event, and step-by-step instructor notes. The guide also contains copies of presentation materials—handouts, presentations, and overhead designs, for example—used in the program.
- *Participant's workbook* Contains exercises and reading materials that support the learning goal and serves as a valuable reference and support guide for participants in the weeks and months that follow the learning event. Typically, each participant will require his or her own workbook.

ELECTRONIC CD-ROMs and web-based products transform static Pfeiffer content into dynamic, interactive experiences. Designed to take advantage of the searchability, automation, and ease-of-use that technology provides, our e-products bring convenience and immediate accessibility to your workspace.

METHODOLOGIES

CASE STUDY A presentation, in narrative form, of an actual event that has occurred inside an organization. Case studies are not prescriptive, nor are they used to prove a point; they are designed to develop critical analysis and decision-making skills. A case study has a specific time frame, specifies a sequence of events, is narrative in structure, and contains a plot structure—an issue (what should be/have been done?). Use case studies when the goal is to enable participants to apply previously learned theories to the circumstances in the case, decide what is pertinent, identify the real issues, decide what should have been done, and develop a plan of action.

ENERGIZER A short activity that develops readiness for the next session or learning event. Energizers are most commonly used after a break or lunch to stimulate or refocus the group. Many involve some form of physical activity, so they are a useful way to counter post-lunch lethargy. Other uses include transitioning from one topic to another, where "mental" distancing is important.

EXPERIENTIAL LEARNING ACTIVITY (ELA) A facilitator-led intervention that moves participants through the learning cycle from experience to application (also known as a Structured Experience). ELAs are carefully thought-out designs in which there is a definite learning purpose and intended outcome. Each step—everything that participants do during the activity—facilitates the accomplishment of the stated goal. Each ELA includes complete instructions for facilitating the intervention and a clear statement of goals, suggested group size and timing, materials required, an explanation of the process, and, where appropriate, possible variations to the activity. (For more detail on Experiential Learning Activities, see the Introduction to the *Reference Guide to Handbooks and Annuals*, 1999 edition, Pfeiffer, San Francisco.)

GAME A group activity that has the purpose of fostering team spirit and togetherness in addition to the achievement of a pre-stated goal. Usually contrived—undertaking a desert expedition, for example—this type of learning method offers an engaging means for participants to demonstrate and practice business and interpersonal skills. Games are effective for team building and personal development mainly because the goal is subordinate to the process—the means through which participants reach decisions, collaborate, communicate, and generate trust and understanding. Games often engage teams in "friendly" competition.

ICEBREAKER A (usually) short activity designed to help participants overcome initial anxiety in a training session and/or to acquaint the participants with one another. An icebreaker can be a fun activity or can be tied to specific topics or training goals. While a useful tool in itself, the icebreaker comes into its own in situations where tension or resistance exists within a group.

INSTRUMENT A device used to assess, appraise, evaluate, describe, classify, and summarize various aspects of human behavior. The term used to describe an instrument depends primarily on its format and purpose. These terms include survey, questionnaire, inventory, diagnostic, survey, and poll. Some uses of instruments include providing instrumental feedback to group members, studying here-and-now processes or functioning within a group, manipulating group composition, and evaluating outcomes of training and other interventions.

Instruments are popular in the training and HR field because, in general, more growth can occur if an individual is provided with a method for focusing specifically on his or her own behavior. Instruments also are used to obtain information that will serve as a basis for change and to assist in workforce planning efforts.

Paper-and-pencil tests still dominate the instrument landscape with a typical package comprising a facilitator's guide, which offers advice on administering the instrument and interpreting the collected data, and an initial set of instruments. Additional instruments are available separately. Pfeiffer, though, is investing heavily in e-instruments. Electronic instrumentation provides effortless distribution and, for larger groups particularly, offers advantages over paper-and-pencil tests in the time it takes to analyze data and provide feedback.

LECTURETTE A short talk that provides an explanation of a principle, model, or process that is pertinent to the participants' current learning needs. A lecturette is intended to establish a common language bond between the trainer and the participants by providing a mutual frame of reference. Use a lecturette as an introduction to a group activity or event, as an interjection during an event, or as a handout.

MODEL A graphic depiction of a system or process and the relationship among its elements. Models provide a frame of reference and something more tangible, and more easily remembered, than a verbal explanation. They also give participants something to "go on," enabling them to track their own progress as they experience the dynamics, processes, and relationships being depicted in the model.

ROLE PLAY A technique in which people assume a role in a situation/scenario: a customer service rep in an angry-customer exchange, for example. The way in which the role is approached is then discussed and feedback is offered. The role play is often repeated using a different approach and/or incorporating changes made based on feedback received. In other words, role playing is a spontaneous interaction involving realistic behavior under artificial (and safe) conditions.

SIMULATION A methodology for understanding the interrelationships among components of a system or process. Simulations differ from games in that they test or use a model that depicts or mirrors some aspect of reality in form, if not necessarily in content. Learning occurs by studying the effects of change on one or more factors of the model. Simulations are commonly used to test hypotheses about what happens in a system—often referred to as "what if?" analysis—or to examine best-case/worst-case scenarios.

THEORY A presentation of an idea from a conjectural perspective. Theories are useful because they encourage us to examine behavior and phenomena through a different lens.

TOPICS

The twin goals of providing effective and practical solutions for workforce training and organization development and meeting the educational needs of training and human resource professionals shape Pfeiffer's publishing program. Core topics include the following:

    Leadership & Management

    Communication & Presentation

    Coaching & Mentoring

    Training & Development

    E-Learning

    Teams & Collaboration

    OD & Strategic Planning

    Human Resources

    Consulting

What will you find on pfeiffer.com?

- The best in workplace performance solutions for training and HR professionals

- Downloadable training tools, exercises, and content

- Web-exclusive offers

- Training tips, articles, and news

- Seamless on-line ordering

- Author guidelines, information on becoming a Pfeiffer Affiliate, and much more

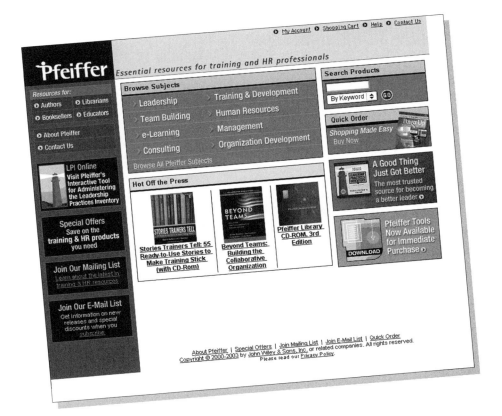

Discover more at www.pfeiffer.com